This book belongs to:

....

Text by Chris Hawkes
Senior Editor James Mitchem
Senior Art Editor Victoria Palastanga
Edited by Hélène Hilton, Becky Walsh
Designed and illustrated by Jim Green, Karen Hood,
Hannah Moore, Rhys Thomas, Sadie Thomas
Design assistance Eleanor Bates
Additional illustrations Shahid Mahmood
Project Picture Researcher Sakshi Saluja
Senior Producer, Pre-Production Tony Phipps
Producer John Casey
Jacket Coordinator Issy Walsh
Creative Technical Support Sonia Charbonnier
Managing Editor Penny Smith
Managing Art Editor Mabel Chan
Publishing Director Sarah Larter
Creative Director Helen Senior

First published in Great Britain in 2020 by
Dorling Kindersley Limited
80 Strand, London, WC2R 0RL

Copyright © 2020 Dorling Kindersley Limited
A Penguin Random House Company
10 9 8 7 6 5 4 3 2 1
001–316217–May/2020

A CIP catalogue record for this book
is available from the British Library.
ISBN: 978-0-2414-0701-1

Printed in China

A WORLD OF IDEAS:
SEE ALL THERE IS TO KNOW

www.dk.com

My Encyclopedia of Very IMPORTANT SPORT

DK

Sports

Sporting **stories**

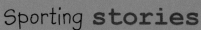

Amazing **athletes**

Sporting **events**

Sports

One of the best things about sports is how many **different ones** there are. There are sports played in snow, in the water, on a special track, or just in the park. There really is a sport for everyone to enjoy, so lace up your trainers and race to find your favourite. **Ready**, **set**, **go**!

American
football

Volleyball

Netball

Basketball

Lacrosse

Handball

Baseball

Hockey

Football

Team sports

Playing in a team is a lot of fun, and team sports are a great way to make friends and develop skills like working **together**. Whether it's throwing, catching, hitting a ball, or scoring goals, the aim of these sports is simple – outscore the other team!

Aussie rules
football

Cricket

Rugby

Football

Known as the "beautiful game", football, or soccer, is the world's most **popular sport**. It's played all over the globe, and its most famous tournament, the World Cup, is the planet's biggest sporting event.

Football pitch

Simple game

The beauty of football is simplicity. Two teams of 11 players play on a pitch with a **goal** at each end. The aim is to kick a ball into the other team's goal. The team with the most goals at the end wins.

Goal

Goalkeeper

Goalkeepers defend the goals. They are the only players who are allowed to touch the ball with their hands.

Inventing the beautiful game

A game similar to football called **Cuju** was played in China more than 2,000 years ago, but the modern game started in England in the 19th century.

> The great thing about football is that it can be played anywhere by anyone. All you need is a ball!

The World Cup

The World Cup decides which country has the best team in the world. It takes place every four years, and the final is watched by **almost half the people on Earth**!

Although professional football is played by teams of 11, it can be played for fun by any number of players.

Three-time World Cup winner Pelé, from Brazil, is one of the game's legends. He scored more than 1,000 goals in his career.

Players per team: 11   Equipment: Ball

American football

In the USA, American football is played at school, college, and professionally in the National Football League (NFL). Each year, the 32 NFL teams square off to win the big prize: the **superbowl**.

Posts

Defensive back

Wide receiver

Get downs

Teams take it in turns to try to get the ball in the other team's **"end zone"** at the end of the field. They get four chances, called **"downs"** to move the ball 10 yards by throwing it or running with it. If the attacking (offensive) team gains 10 yards they get four more downs. If they fail, the other team gets the ball.

Type of sport:  Ball

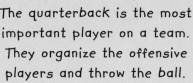

The quarterback throws the ball to their team's RECEIVERS.

Touchdown!

Teams score six points if they run the ball into the other team's end zone, or successfully catch the ball there. This is called a **touchdown**. Teams also score three points if they kick the ball between the posts for a **field goal**.

The quarterback is the most important player on a team. They organize the offensive players and throw the ball.

American football players wear lots of **pads** and a helmet to protect them when they get tackled.

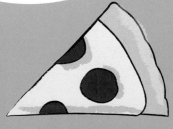

Quarterback

The American football ball is called a "pigskin".

Professional teams have 53 players on a squad, but only 11 on each side play at once.

More pizza is sold in the United States on the day of the Superbowl than any other day of the year!

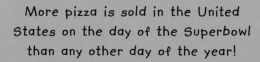

Players per team: 11

Equipment: Protective clothing, helmet, ball

Australian rules football

Australian rules football is a very physical ball sport popular in **Australia**. It's played between two teams of 18 players.

The game can be rough, and players don't wear pads or a helmet, so need to be very tough.

Scoring

Teams move a ball around a big pitch by kicking it, running and bouncing it, or thumping it with their fists. They score points by kicking the ball between goal posts — **six points** for the middle posts, and **one point** for the wider "behind" posts.

The game is also known as "Aussie rules" or just "footy".

FACT FILE

Type of sport: Ball

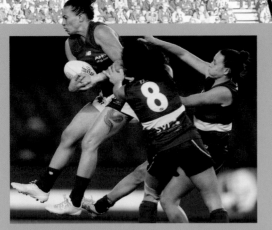

Even though women's games have been played since the 1910s, the official women's league only played its first season in 2017.

	Goals	Behinds	Points
Team 1	11	14	80
Team 2	10	7	67

The sport was invented as a game for cricketers to play during winter when the weather wasn't good enough for cricket.

Australian rules football is played on an oval pitch

Funny scoring

A scoreboard might read: 11.14 (80), 10.7 (67). This means that Team 1 scored 80 points (11 goals and 14 behinds), while Team 2 scored 67 points (10 goals and 7 behinds).

Players per team: 18

Equipment: Ball

Rugby

Rugby can be tough. It helps to be big, fast, and strong.

Rugby is a team sport where players pass and kick an **oval-shaped** ball. The aim is to score more points than the other team.

OUCH!

Teams move the ball by passing it to a teammate or by kicking it. Players are only allowed to pass the ball backwards. The defending team tackles players to take the ball from them.

If a team places the ball on the ground behind the other team's "try line", it scores a "try" and earns points. Teams also score points if they kick the ball between the goal posts.

FACT FILE

Types of rugby

15 **Rugby union** is a 15-a-side version of the game. According to myth, it started in 1823, when a pupil at a school in Rugby, England, picked up the ball during a game of football and ran with it.

13 **Rugby league** is similar to rugby union, but teams have 13 players and the points for scoring are different.

7 **Sevens** is a seven-a-side version of rugby union. A match is made up of two halves lasting for seven minutes each.

If a player passes the ball forwards, a "scrum" occurs. In a scrum, the teams lock shoulders and push against each other. The ball is rolled into the middle and both teams struggle to get it.

After a try is scored, the team tries to kick the ball between the goal posts to earn more points. That's why it's called a "try".

 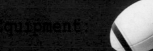

Lacrosse

Lacrosse is a team sport where players **run**, **pass** a ball, **catch** it, and score using **sticks** with a net at the end.

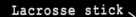
Lacrosse stick

Body checking

Lacrosse is similar to many team sports in that the aim is to **score goals** in the other team's net. When the other team has the ball, one way to get it back is to "body check" a player so they drop the ball. This means slamming into them!

Battle ready

Lacrosse is based on a game played in Native American communities, often to **prepare warriors for battle**. The game could last for days and sometimes included up to 1,000 players!

FACT FILE Type of sport: Stick and ball

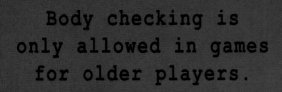

Body checking is only allowed in games for older players.

Fast and furious

Lacrosse is a very tough and physical sport. Players need to be covered in **protective clothing**, including a helmet, shoulder guards, gloves, arm pads, and body armour.

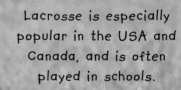

Lacrosse is especially popular in the USA and Canada, and is often played in schools.

Baseball

Baseball is played between two teams of nine players who take turns **batting** and **fielding**. It's hugely popular in North America, Japan, and South Korea.

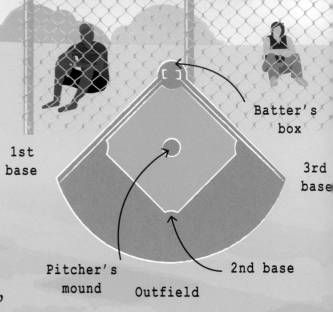

1st base

Batter's box

3rd base

Pitcher's mound

2nd base

Outfield

A baseball pitch is called a "diamond" because of its shape.

Batter up!

The game starts when **the pitcher** throws the ball towards a **batter**. The batter tries to hit the ball and sprint around **four bases** to score a **"run"**. It's the fielding team's job to get the batter out.

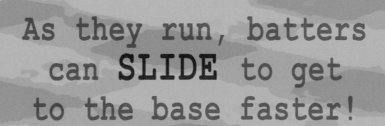

As they run, batters can **SLIDE** to get to the base faster!

FACT FILE   Type of sport: Bat and ball

Three strikes and you're out!

Home run glory

If a player hits the ball out of the field, it's a home run. This means the player can run freely around **all four bases** to score.

Out!

There are a few ways the fielders can get a **batter out**:

 If the pitcher throws three strikes (makes the batter miss the ball three times).

 If a fielder catches the ball before it touches the ground.

 If the ball is thrown to a fielder standing on a base before the batter reaches it.

← Baseball glove

Over 21 million hot dogs were eaten at baseball stadiums in the USA in 2014.

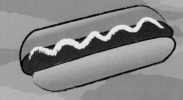

Players per team: 9

Equipment:  Bat, ball, glove, helmet

Cricket

Cricket is a bat-and-ball game popular in many countries. The aim of the game is to score more **runs** than the other team.

Fielders are a team's defenders. It's their job to catch the batsmen "out".

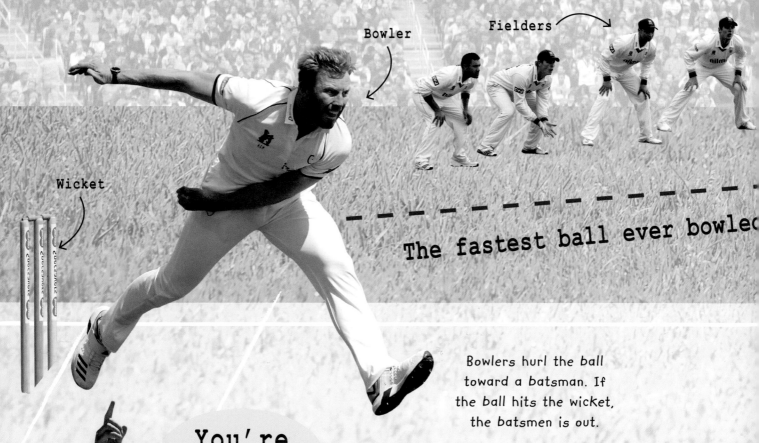

Bowler

Fielders

Wicket

The fastest ball ever bowled

Bowlers hurl the ball toward a batsman. If the ball hits the wicket, the batsmen is out.

You're out!

Two umpires make sure the match is fair and decide whether a batsman is out.

Cricket pitch
The game is played on a big field, in the centre of which is a pitch that has **wickets** at both ends.

FACT FILE   Type of sport: 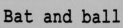 Bat and ball

One of cricket's biggest rivalries is between England and Australia. They play for a tiny trophy called The Ashes. It's the smallest trophy in sport!

Aim of the game

One team scores runs when one of its batsmen **strikes the ball** with the bat. It's the other team's job to **get the batsman out**. There are lots of ways to do this, including catching a hit ball before it touches the ground.

Bat

Wicket

was at 161kph (100mph)

Pads

Ball

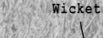

Cricket is extremely popular in India, Pakistan, and the West Indies.

Players per team: 11

Equipment: 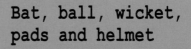 Bat, ball, wicket, pads and helmet

Hockey

Hockey, also called "field hockey", is a game where players use curved, **wooden sticks** to hit a ball to their teammates and try to **score goals**.

Matches are usually played on artificial

Players can only hit the ball with the flat side of the stick.

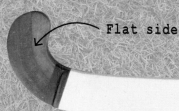

Flat side

FACT FILE   Type of sport:    Stick and ball

Players are not allowed to touch the ball with their hands or feet.

Goalkeepers wear protective padding from head to toe.

Shinty is an old Scottish game similar to hockey.

The Wizard

India's **Dhyan Chand** is one of the greatest hockey players ever. He was known as **"The Wizard"** because of his amazing control of the ball. His team dominated men's hockey in the 1920s and 1930s, and won three Olympic golds in a row between 1928 and 1936.

Origins

From ancient Greece to ancient China, games in which a ball is hit with a stick have been played for a very long time. But hockey as we know it developed in **Scotland** around 300 years ago.

Handle

grass as it's smoother than real grass.

Basketball

Fast-paced and exciting, basketball is a popular team sport where two teams compete to shoot a ball into **baskets**.

Basket

The first basketball hoops were baskets peaches were sold in!

Basketball court

Free throw line

Three point line

Basket

If a player is fouled while shooting, their team is given undefended shots from the "free throw" line.

Type of sport: Ball

28

Shoot!

Getting the ball in the other team's hoop earns points. Shots from outside the **three point line** are worth three points, and scores from inside it are worth two.

Michael Jordan is basketball's biggest legend. He averaged 30.1 points a game across his career.

Slam dunk in action!

Leaping and slamming the ball into the basket is called a slam dunk.

The world's most famous basketball league, the NBA is in the United States, but basketball is popular across Europe and Asia, too.

Basketball players are fast, skilful, and big. NBA legend Shaquille O'Neal is 7ft 1in (2.16m) tall, and wears size 22 shoes!

Average man's shoe size

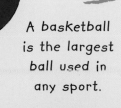

Shaquille O'Neal's shoe size

A basketball is the largest ball used in any sport.

Netball

Netball is a team sport similar to basketball. Players pass a ball to each other and try to **shoot the ball** through one of two raised rings at each end of the court.

It's the goal keeper's job to protect their team's goal.

Beginning of the sport

Netball began as a version of basketball that was played by women **students** at a college in London. The first rules were made in 1901 and the sport grew from there.

The Netball World Cup is the sport's biggest event. Australia have won 11 times and never finished lower than second place.

FACT FILE   Type of sport:    Ball

Only the goal attack and goal shooter are allowed to enter the other team's goal circle and try to score.

Goal circle

Players are given positions that define what their job on the team is. Only some positions are allowed to go to certain parts of the court.

GK	**GD**	**WD**	**C**	**WA**	**GA**	**GS**
Goal keeper	Goal defence	Wing defence	Centre	Wing attack	Goal attack	Goal Shooter

Rules of netball
The aim of netball is to get the ball into the other team's hoop.

1 Players have letters on them to show the positions they take on the court.

2 Players are not allowed to run with or bounce the ball, and must pass the ball or shoot within three seconds of receiving it.

3 Shots can only be made from inside a special area called the goal circle. Only the goal attack and goal shooter can enter it.

4 Defenders must stay at least 1m (3ft) away from a player who has the ball.

5 Matches last for 60 minutes. The team with the most goals at the end of the game wins.

60 mins

Players per team: 7   **Equipment:** Ball and ring

Volleyball

Volleyball is played between two teams separated by a **tall net**. The teams hit the ball over the net until one team can't return it.

Indoor volleyball has been played at the Olympics since the 1964 Games in Tokyo, Japan.

Teaching volleyball

Volleyball was invented by American teacher William G. Morgan in 1895. He combined parts of **tennis**, **handball**, and **basketball** to create a game that would keep his students fit.

Volleyball is played regularly by more than 800 million people around the world.

Most volleyball players jump around 300 times during a match.

FACT FILE   Type of sport:    Ball

Over the net

Teams knock the ball back and forth over the net. Each team can touch the ball **three times** before returning it, but players are not allowed to touch the ball twice in a row. If the ball touches the ground, or a team fails to return the ball into the opponent's court, the other team wins a point.

"Jenny" Lang Ping of China is a volleyball legend as both a player and a coach.

After retiring as a player, I coached the Chinese and US teams.

Net

Beach volleyball

Beach volleyball is a **two-a-side** version of volleyball played on sand. It has been played at the Olympic Games since 1996.

Handball

Handball is a fast-paced ball game played between two teams of seven players. The aim is to move the ball around the pitch and **throw it** into the other team's goal.

Handball is very popular in Europe. Especially in France, Germany, Spain, and Sweden.

The game's first rules were written in 1906 by Danish sports teacher and Olympian, Holger Nielsen.

Moving around

To move the ball, players can **pass** it to each other, **run** with it, or **shoot**! If a player runs with the ball, they must bounce it as they run (dribble with it).

Dribbling

Passing

World Championships

The handball World Championships are held every two years. **France** have won the men's event six times, and **Russia** holds the record in the women's with four wins.

Scoring goals

The goal is surrounded by a 6m (20ft) **zone**, in which only the goalkeeper is allowed. Goals have to be scored from outside the zone or while jumping into it.

FACT FILE

Type of sport:	Players per team:	Equipment:
Ball	7	Ball and goal

35

Mountaineering

Triathlon

Squash

Tai chi

Athletics

Taekwondo

Golf

Karate

Dressage

Table tennis

Tennis

Archery

Gymnastics

Cycling

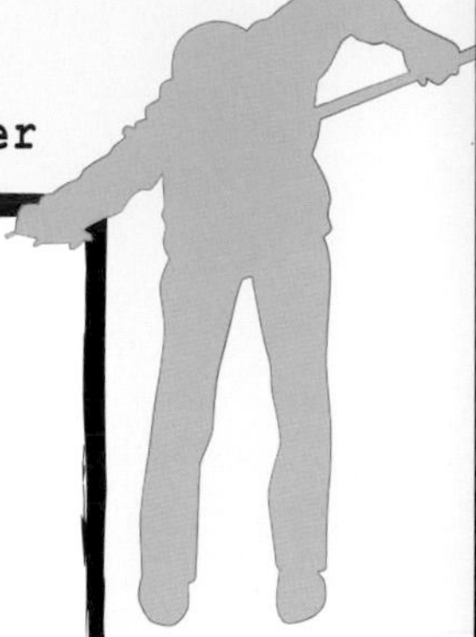

Individual sports

There are lots of solo sports to choose from, and they all require very different **skills**. Players mostly compete on their own, but some can be played in pairs or a small team. Hop, skip, and jump over the page to learn more.

Snooker

Fencing

Skateboarding

Badminton

Darts

Bowling

Horse racing

Formula One

Ancient sports

People have played sports since ancient times, as a way of having fun and as competition. Some ancient sports are **still played today**!

Kabaddi

This game is played by two teams of seven. One player, known as the "raider", runs into the other team's half of the court, tags as many opponents as possible, and gets back to their own half without being tackled.

Polo

First played in Persia (now Iran) in the sixth century BCE, polo is one of the world's oldest team sports. Players on horses try to hit a ball into an opponent's goal with a hammer.

Pitch-pot

In this ancient game from East Asia, players try to throw long sticks or arrows into a jar or pot from a distance.

Wrestling

This combat sport is all about overpowering the opponent by grappling, throwing, and pinning them down. It was painted on cave walls 15,000 years ago, and is still played!

Jousting

In this medieval sport, two riders charge at each other on horseback while holding a long stick called a "lance". The aim is to knock your opponent off their horse.

Nguni stick-fighting

In this ancient African martial art, two players fight each other with two sticks. One stick is used to attack; the other is used to defend.

Episkyros

In this ancient Greek ball game, players pass a ball to a teammate standing behind the other team's goal line. It's a little like American football.

Chunkey

This Native American game was first played 1,500 years ago. One player rolls a stone disc across the ground while others throw spears and try to hit it.

Chunkey stone

Cuju

Played in China from the third century BCE, this is thought to be one of the earliest forms of football.

Running

From fast sprints to long-distance endurance races, there are lots of running events in athletics. Running short distances requires explosive **speed**, while athletes who run long distances need energy and **stamina**.

Sprints and distances

The distances for running at the **Olympics** are divided into sprints, middle-distance, and long-distance races. They are:

100m	200m	400m	800m
The shortest running event takes place on the straight section of an athletics track. Jamaica's Usain Bolt broke the world record in 2009.	Athletes start the 200m race on the curve of a track and finish on a straight. USA's Florence Griffith-Joyner set the women's record in 1988 and it's never been beaten.	This race takes place around a full lap of the track. Runners either start quickly and try to keep a good pace, or increase their speed near the end.	The shortest of the middle-distance races, the 800m requires both stamina and speed. Athletes run two laps of the track.
Usain Bolt	Florence Griffith-Joyner		David Rudisha

Current world records

Distance	Men	Women
100m	Usain Bolt, Jamaica 9.58 seconds (2009)	Florence Griffith Joyner, USA 10.49 seconds (1988)
200m	Usain Bolt, Jamaica 19.19 seconds (2009)	Florence Griffith Joyner, USA 21.34 seconds (1988)
400m	Wayde van Niekerk, South Africa 43.03 seconds (2016)	Marita Koch, East Germany 47.60 seconds (1985)
800m	David Rudisha, Kenya 1 minute, 40.91 seconds (2012)	Jarmila Kratochvílová, Czechoslovakia 1 minute, 53.28 seconds (1983)
1500m	Hicham El Guerrouj, Morocco 3 minutes, 26.00 seconds (1998)	Genzebe Dibaba, Ethiopia 3 minutes, 50.07 seconds (2015)
5000m	Kenenisa Bekele, Ethiopia 12 minutes, 37.35 seconds (2004)	Tirunesh Dibaba, Ethiopia 14 minutes, 11.15 seconds (2008)
10000m	Kenenisa Bekele, Ethiopia 26 minutes, 17.53 seconds (2005)	Almaz Ayana, Ethiopia 29 minutes, 17.45 seconds (2016)
Marathon	Eliud Kipchoge, Kenya 2 hours, 1 minute, 39 seconds (2018)	Brigid Kosgei, Kenya 2 hours, 14 minutes, 4 seconds (2019)

1500m	5000m	10000m	Marathon
This race covers three-and-a-quarter laps of a track. The best athletes run the race as a long sprint.	This is the shortest long-distance race and covers 12-and-a-half laps of a track.	Athletes must complete 25 laps of the track. The event has been part of the Olympics for men since 1912, and for women since 1988.	The marathon is the longest event. Instead of running on a track, athletes race over a road course that is 42.195km (26.219 miles) long.
Hicham El Guerrouj	Kenenisa Bekele	Almaz Ayana	Brigid Kosgei

Hurdles

Four athletics events involve jumping over **obstacles**. Women run the 100m hurdles, while men run 110m. Both compete in a 400m hurdles race and a 3000m steeplechase, with special obstacles.

Steeplechase is the human version of a type of horse race. Obstacles include tall barriers and water pits.

The hurdles are set at different heights, depending on the race.

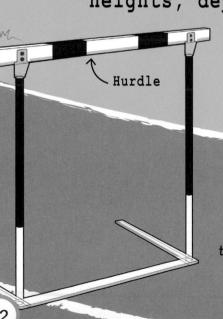

← Hurdle

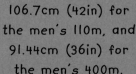

106.7cm (42in) for the men's 110m, and 91.44cm (36in) for the men's 400m.

83.8cm (33in) for the women's 100m, and 76.2cm (30in) for the women's 400m.

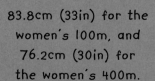

91.4cm (36in) in the men's steeplechase, and 76.2cm (30in) in women's.

Master hurdler

American Ed Moses was top of the men's 400m hurdles for a decade. He won **122 races in a row** between 1977 and 1987, picking up four world records and two Olympic gold medals.

World records

Distance	Men	Women
100m hurdles	No event	Kendra Harrison, USA 12.20 seconds (2016)
110m hurdles	Aries Merritt, USA 12.80 seconds (2012)	No event
400m hurdles	Kevin Young, USA 46.78 seconds (1992)	Dalilah Muhammad, USA 52.16 seconds (2019)
3000m steeplechase	Saif Saaeed Shaheen, Qatar 7 minutes, 53.63 seconds (2004)	Beatrice Chepkoech, Kenya 8 minutes, 44.32 seconds (2018)

Top long jumpers leap further than a London bus!

Jumps

In athletics, there are four events where **jumping** is key: long jump, high jump, triple jump, and pole vault.

High jump

Flip

Athletes jump over a bar onto a mat. If they clear the bar, it is moved higher. If they don't clear it in three tries, they are eliminated. The winner is whoever jumps highest.

Long jump

Leap

In long jump, athletes sprint down a runway then to leap as far as they can into a sand pit. The winner is whoever leaps furthest.

Triple jump

Hop...

Skip...

World records

Event	Men	Women
High jump	Javier Sotomayor, Cuba 2.45m (1993)	Stefka Kostadinova, Bulgaria 2.09m (1987)
Long jump	Mike Powell, USA 8.95m (1991)	Galina Chistyakova, USSR 7.52m (1988)
Triple jump	Jonathan Edwards, GB 18.29m (1995)	Inessa Kravets, Ukraine 15.50m (1995)
Pole vault	Renaud Lavillenie, France 6.16m (2014)	Yelena Isinbayeva, Russia 5.06m (2009)

Pole vault

Just as in high jump, pole vaulters have to leap over a bar. But they use a long stick to help them get over the bar.

Ukraine's Sergey Bubka broke the pole vault world record 35 times between 1984 and 2001!

Sergey Bubka →

Jump

Triple jump is similar to the long jump, but athletes must hop, skip, then jump. The winner is the athlete who gets the furthest.

Throws

There are four throwing events in athletics: **shot put**, **discus**, **javelin**, and **hammer**. In each event the athlete who throws the furthest wins.

Discus

Shot

Shot put

Athletes throw a small, heavy metal ball called a "**shot**" as far as they can, while staying inside a special throwing circle.

Discus is an ancient sport. There are statues of people throwing a discus that date back more than 2,000 years.

Discus

Athletes spin around to gain speed, then throw a **metal disc** (the discus) as far as possible. As with shot put, competitors have to stay in a special circle while throwing.

Javelin

Javelin is the only throwing event in which athletes don't stay in a throwing circle. They sprint down a runway and release the javelin (a **spear**) through the air.

Hammer

Hammer

The hammer isn't like a hammer you would find in a toolbox. It's a **metal ball** attached to a steel wire. Athletes spin around in a throwing circle, build up speed, then let it go.

Javelin

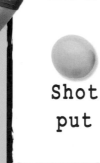

Shot put

Hammer

Javelin

Discus

Event	Men	Women
Shot put	Randy Barnes, USA 23.12m (1990)	Natalya Lisovskaya, USSR 22.63m (1987)
Discus	Jürgen Schult, East Germany 74.08m (1986)	Gabriele Reinsch, East Germany 76.80m (1988)
Javelin	Jan Železný, Czech Republic 98.48m (1996)	Barbora Špotáková, Czech Republic 72.28m (2008)
Hammer	Yuriy Sedykh, USSR 86.74m (1986)	Anita Włodarczyk, Poland 82.98m (2016)

Combined events

Combined events are the **ultimate test** of an athlete's abilities, as they compete in lots of events to decide the winner. Men compete in the **decathlon**, while women compete in the **heptathlon**.

I FRANCE
TDK
MAYER
LONDON 2017

Decathlon world record
Kevin Mayer, France
9,126 points (2018)

Decathlon
The decathlon has **ten events**:

100m   Long jump   Shot put   High jump   400m

110m hurdles   Discus   Pole vault   Javelin   1500m

Heptathlon

The heptathlon has **seven events**:

100m hurdles   High jump   Shot put

200m   Long jump   Javelin   800m

The heptathlon was first part of the OLYMPIC GAMES in 1984.

Scoring

Athletes score points for the time, height, or distance they achieve in each event. The points are added up and the athlete with the most points at the end wins.

Triathlon

A triathlon is an endurance race where athletes **swim**, **cycle**, then **run**, one after the other. People who take part in triathlons must train very hard!

How it all started

Multi-sport events have been around since ancient times, but **nobody really knows** the origins of the modern triathlon. However, the first official swim-cycle-run competition was held in the USA in 1974, and was the first to be officially called a triathlon.

Triathlon is a mix of two Greek words, "tri" and "athlos", which mean "three competitions".

Olympic triathlon

Triathlon became an Olympic event at the 2000 Olympics in Sydney, Australia. Competitors complete a 1.5km (0.93 mile) swim, followed by a 40km (25 mile) cycle, then a 10km (6.2 mile) run.

FACT FILE   Type of sport: Endurance

Brilliant Brownlee

Britain's Alistair Brownlee is the only triathlete in history to win **back to back** Olympic titles. He won gold at the 2012 Games in London, England, and then again at Rio de Janeiro, Brazil, four years later.

Alistair Brownlee

There are variations of the classic triathlon. One features cross-country skiing, mountain biking, and running.

In 2018, Hiromu Inada from Japan became the oldest person to complete an Ironman. He did it at the age of 85!

Made of iron

There are several extreme versions of triathlons. The most famous is called an **Ironman**. In this race, competitors swim 3.9km (2.4 miles), cycle 180km (112 miles), and then run 42.2 km (26.2 miles).

The record for an Ironman is held by Germany's Jan Frodeno. He completed the event in 7 hours, 35 minutes, 39 seconds.

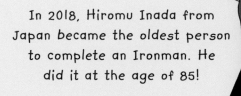

Number of players: 1

Equipment: Running shoes, swimwear, bicycle

Gymnastics

Gymnasts make incredibly difficult **acrobatics** look effortless. There are lots of events, but they all require strength, flexibility, balance, and stamina.

Balance beam

Gymnasts perform jumps, flips, and twists on a thin wooden beam without falling off.

Beam →

Pommel horse

The pommel horse is a box with handles on it. Gymnasts use the horse to spin on their hands, do scissor kicks, and handstands.

Most gymnasts start training when they are very young.

Uneven bars

Without touching the floor, gymnasts spin, do handstands and jumps on two bars set at different heights.

Floor exercise

Gymnasts show their acrobatic skills on a spring floor mat by performing balances, jumps, flips, leaps, and turns.

FACT FILE   Type of sport: 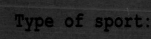   Gymnastics

Gymnastics has appeared at every Olympics since 1896. Men and women compete in slightly different events.

Parallel bars

Gymnasts use two bars to perform a series of swings, balances, and spins.

Rings

Gymnasts lift themselves off the ground on the rings, and use their strength to spin and hold different positions.

Vault

After a short run-up, gymnasts jump onto a springboard, place their hands on a vault, throw themselves up into the air, and perform flips.

Trampolining

In trampolining, gymnasts bounce in the air as they spin and twirl. Competitions can be for one gymnast or pairs.

Rhythmic gymnastics

This is a mix of dance, gymnastics, and ballet. Rhythmic gymnasts perform routines with props such as balls, hoops, ribbons, clubs, or a skipping rope.

Number of players: 1–4

Equipment: Beam, pommel horse, bars, rings, and more

Cycling

People ride bikes for fun or to get around, but competitive cycling takes it up a level. There are lots of different races that take place on **roads** or on indoor tracks called **velodromes**.

Cycling's biggest races are known as the "Grand Tours". The most well-known, the Tour de France, lasts for three weeks!

Cycling races can be quick sprints, or endurance races that take a long time and lots of stamina.

SPRINT RACES

SPRINT

These races are mostly between two cyclists who race over a set distance, usually between 250m-1000m.

KEIRIN

In this six-lap race, riders have to stay behind a motor cycle for the first three laps, then are released to race over the last three.

TEAM SPRINT

This is a three-person team time trial. Teams try to record the fastest time.

TIME TRIAL

Each rider tries to record the fastest time over a set distance.

ENDURANCE RACES

INDIVIDUAL PURSUIT

Two cyclists start on opposite ends of a track. If one rider catches the other, the race is over. If neither catches the other, the one with the fastest time wins.

SCRATCH RACE

In this race, all the riders start together and race. The winner is the first to cross the finishing line.

FACT FILE

Type of sport: Cycling

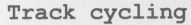

Road races

Single cyclists or teams take part in races on roads. Some are staged over **several laps** of a course, some take a day, and others are **multi-stage** races that take much longer.

Track cycling

Track cycling events take place in a purpose-built velodrome. The tracks usually have two flat straights with slanted turns at either end to help the cyclists go **faster**.

TEAM PURSUIT

Just like the individual pursuit, cyclists chase each other around a track, but in teams of up to four riders.

MADISON

This is a team-relay event. The winning team is the one that completes the most laps in a set time.

MISS AND OUT

This is an elimination race in which the slowest riders are eliminated until only the winner is left.

POINTS RACE

These can be complicated to watch. A sprint is held every ten laps and the first five riders in each sprint collect points. The rider with the most points wins.

OMNIUM

This is a multi-stage event, involving several kinds of race in one. The winner is the rider who gets the most overall points.

Number of players: 1 or team

Equipment: Bicycle, helmet

Formula One

Formula One is a fast, thrilling racing sport. Drivers race and are awarded points for the position they finish in. The driver with the most points at the end of the season is the **champion**.

A Formula One car can cost $10 million!

↖ Monaco Grand Prix

Fast-paced racing

Races are called "Grand Prix", which means **"large prize"** in French. Each Grand Prix is held on a different track, which can vary a lot. For example, the Monaco Grand Prix is held around twisty streets, while the Italian Grand Prix has long straights to speed along.

FACT FILE   Type of sport: Motor

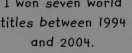

I won seven world titles between 1994 and 2004.

Germany's Michael Schumacher is the most successful driver in the history of the sport.

Pit stops

During races, drivers pull into special "pit stops" where a team changes all their tyres in seconds! A good pit stop makes the difference between **winning or losing** the race.

←Pit stop

Officials wave a chequered flag to show when the winner crosses the finish line.

Built for speed

Formula One cars can reach speeds of 375 kph (235 mph). They are specially designed to generate **"downforce"**, which helps them stay on the ground when they go around corners at such high speeds.

Motor sports

There are lots of sports where man and machine come together with one goal in mind: going as **fast as possible**!

↑

Lewis Hamilton

Go-karting

Many Formula One drivers, such as Lewis Hamilton, start off racing go-karts. Drivers race around tracks in small powerful karts.

Touring car racing

Drivers race everyday cars that have been modified, around race tracks. Some touring car races last a whole day!

Motorcycle racing

Riders drive high-powered motorcycles around tracks or road circuits at super speeds.

Drag racing

The ultimate test of speed. Drag racers drive cars designed to go as fast as possible in a straight line over a short distance.

Speedway

Between four to six riders race motorcycles around a short, dirt track.

Monster truck

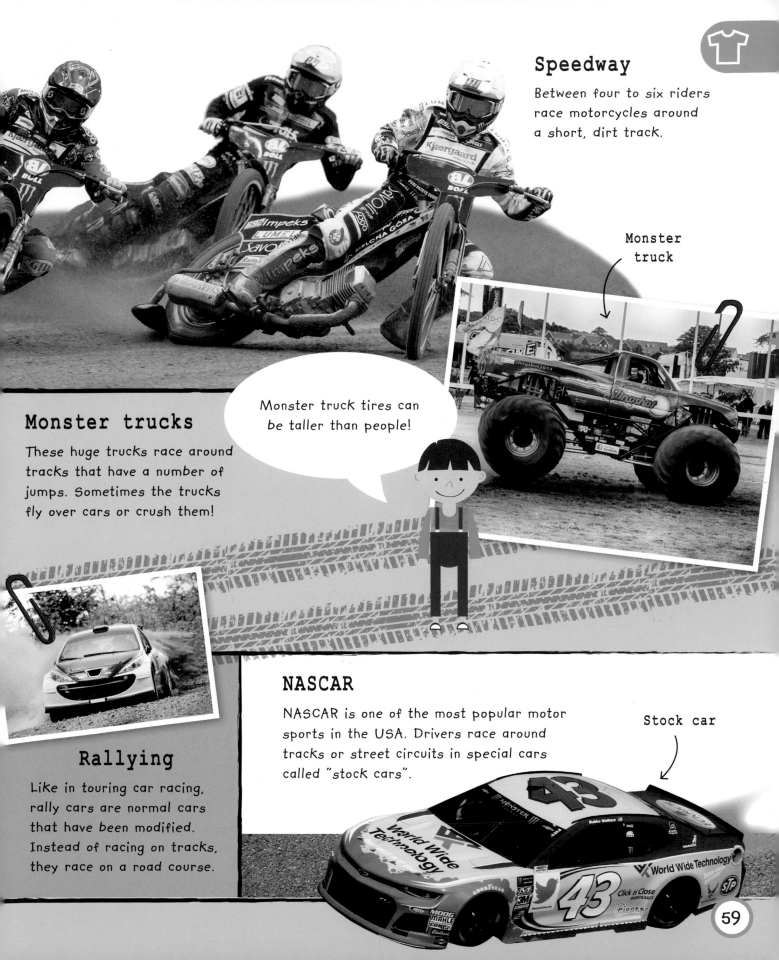

Monster trucks

These huge trucks race around tracks that have a number of jumps. Sometimes the trucks fly over cars or crush them!

Monster truck tires can be taller than people!

Rallying

Like in touring car racing, rally cars are normal cars that have been modified. Instead of racing on tracks, they race on a road course.

NASCAR

NASCAR is one of the most popular motor sports in the USA. Drivers race around tracks or street circuits in special cars called "stock cars".

Stock car

Horse racing

Horse racing is one of the **oldest** sports there is. Riders called **jockeys** race horses around a track as fast as possible.

Flat races

In flat races, horses gallop around a **track**. Some of the world's most famous horse races, such as the Kentucky Derby, are flat races.

Kentucky Derby

The Kentucky Derby is called the "Fastest Two Minutes in Sports".

FACT FILE   Type of sport: Equestrian

Jump races

Also known as "steeplechase", jump races also take place on a track, but horses must jump over **obstacles**, such as fences and ditches.

Steeplechase jump

Steeplechasing gets its name from races that took place between two church steeples.

Jockeys are SMALL AND LIGHT, it helps the horses RUN FASTER.

Most races are run anti-clockwise around the track.

Showjumping

Equestrian events are competitions for **horses** and **riders**. The most well-known is showjumping.

Showjumping

Showjumping is an **obstacle course** for horses and riders. Horses have to leap over hedges and walls. Riders lose points if their horse is too slow or knocks over an obstacle.

Neighhhh!

Jump

FACT FILE Type of sport: Equestrian

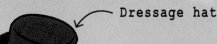
Dressage hat

Dressage

Dressage horses perform **special steps** and moves to show how well they follow instructions from their rider.

Aaaachoo!

British rider Lee Pearson has won ten dressage gold medals at the Paralympics even though he is allergic to horses!

Dance steps

Dressage gets its name from the French word for **"training"**. It takes a lot of time and skill to train a horse to be obedient enough for dressage. Some dressage events are performed to **music**, just like a dance.

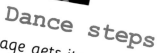

Dressage is sometimes called "horse ballet".

Combat sports

There are lots of sports where opponents face each other in a **one-on-one** fight. Most were created years ago in different cultures around the world.

Boxing gloves

Kendo shinai

Krav Maga

This martial art was developed by the Israeli army. It is a mix of boxing, wrestling, aikido, judo, and karate.

Kendo

Kendo is a Japanese martial art where fighters wear protective armour and use bamboo swords called "shinai" to fight each other.

Judo

The goal in judo is to grapple and throw your opponent to the ground and pin them there. It was invented in Japan.

Boxing

Boxing is one of the world's oldest combat sports. It's also called "pugilism". Boxers wear padded gloves on their hands.

POW

Even though they involve fighting, most martial arts

Ring

Sumo wrestling

Sumo wrestling is Japan's national sport. Wrestlers must force their opponents out of a ring or throw them to the ground to win.

Aikido

This Japanese martial art has its roots in the 12th century, but its modern form was developed in the early 20th century. It is mainly used for self-defence.

Hakama

Capoeira

This is an African-Brazilian martial art that developed in Brazil in the 16th century. It combines elements of dance, acrobatics, and music.

Kickboxing

Kickboxing developed as a mix of karate and boxing. There are lots of different styles from different countries.

Mixed martial arts

This sport uses techniques from lots of different martial arts. It combines grappling and striking.

Kung Fu

"Kung Fu" refers to the Chinese martial arts. Monks invented Kung Fu as a way to train their bodies for meditation.

are meant for self-defence.

Karate

Karate is a **martial art** (form of self-defense) that uses punching, kicking, and hand strikes. Karate originated on the Japanese island of Okinawa in the 19th century and later became a popular sport.

Karategi

Obi

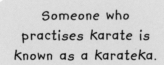

Someone who practises karate is known as a karateka.

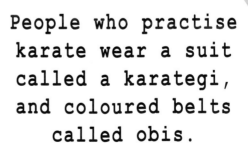

People who practise karate wear a suit called a karategi, and coloured belts called obis.

Origins

In the 17th century, fighting with weapons was banned on Okinawa, so its warriors came up with karate. The word karate means "**empty hand**".

Karate's popularity spread to the United States when Okinawa became an important US military base after World War II.

Gaining belts

As karateka improve at karate, they pass through several ranks (**dans**). Each dan has a different coloured belt. Beginners start with white, and experts wear black.

Types of move

Karate is known for striking actions such as palm heel, knife hand, and spear hand strikes. But karate is mostly about self-defence and developing **balance** between the mind and body.

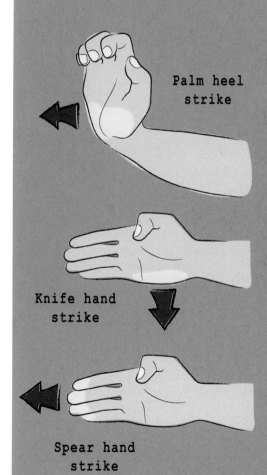

Palm heel strike

Knife hand strike

Spear hand strike

 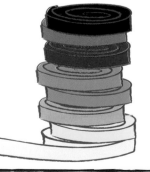

Taekwondo

Taekwondo is a martial art and form of self-defence based on speed, agility, and acrobatic **kicks**.

Origins

Taekwondo developed in **South Korea** from a number of different Korean, Japanese, and Chinese martial arts that date back more than **2,000** years.

People who take part in Taekwondo are expected to follow the following five tenets (rules).

Courtesy

Integrity

Perseverance

Self-control

Indomitable spirit

"Tae" means foot, "kwon" mean fist, and "do" translates to "art" or "the way".

The Taekwondo uniform is called a "DOBOK".

FACT FILE   Type of sport: Martial art

Contestants perform in weight categories, so they always fight against someone who is a similar size to them.

Competitions

Contestants wear a red or blue chest protector (called a **hogu**), a head guard, and other forms of protection. The contest is made up of **three rounds** of two minutes. The person who scores the most points wins.

Taekwondo first appeared at the Olympics in Sydney, Australia, in 2000. South Korea have won more medals than any other country.

← Hogu

3 **How to win points** **5**

One point for a foot or fist strike that hits the body

Three points for a kick to the head

Three points for a spinning or back kick that strikes the body

Four points for a spinning kick to the head

Tai chi

This very old martial art uses slow **flowing movements**, deep breathing, and meditation to exercise the body and clear the mind.

Ancient art

Tai chi began in **China** hundreds of years ago. According to legend, a monk named Zhang Sanfeng came upon a fight between a snake and a bird. The way the animals moved inspired him to create tai chi.

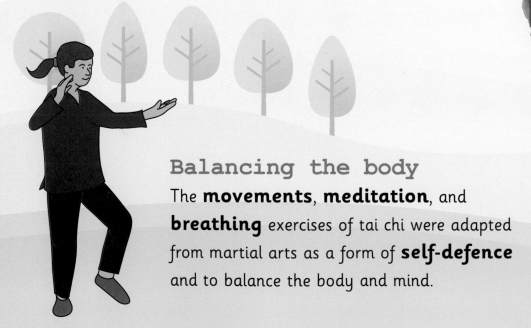

Balancing the body

The **movements**, **meditation**, and **breathing** exercises of tai chi were adapted from martial arts as a form of **self-defence** and to balance the body and mind.

FACT FILE   Type of sport: Martial art

More than 10 million people practise tai chi daily in China. It's one of the world's most popular ways to exercise.

There are five styles of tai chi. They are named after the five families who created them.

Routines

The type and **number of moves** in a tai chi routine depends on the style of tai chi. Some forms have around **20** movements, and others have up to **150**.

 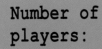

Fencing

Fencing is a safe version of **sword fighting**.
It's based on the ancient art of swordsmanship, but
the modern rules date back to 19th century Europe.

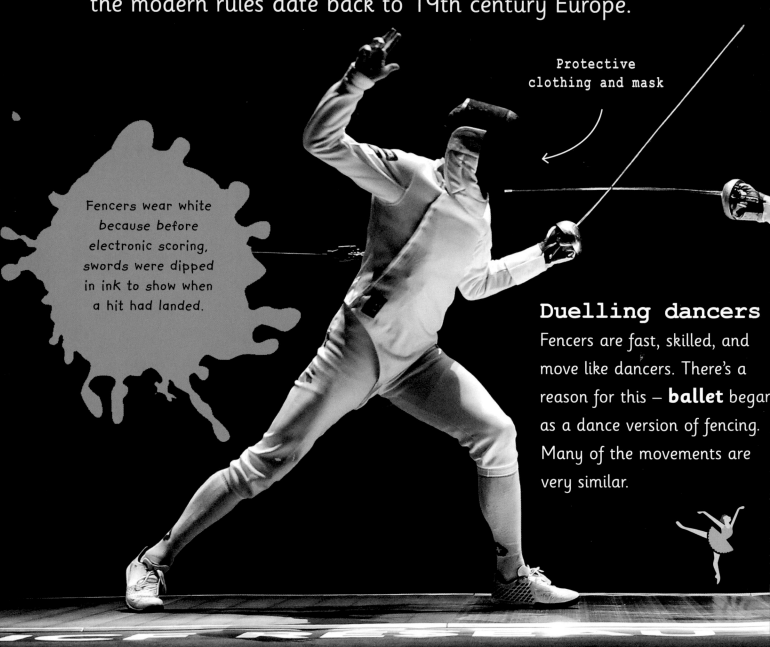

Protective
clothing and mask

Fencers wear white
because before
electronic scoring,
swords were dipped
in ink to show when
a hit had landed.

Duelling dancers
Fencers are fast, skilled, and
move like dancers. There's a
reason for this – **ballet** began
as a dance version of fencing.
Many of the movements are
very similar.

FACT FILE   Type of sport: Combat

Forms of fencing

There are three different forms of fencing, depending on the weapon being used: the **foil**, the **épée**, or the **sabre**. The aim is the same in all of them — win points by touching the opponent with the sword.

Contact is detected electronically using a special cord. A sound is made or a light comes on when a touch is made.

Cord

Foil

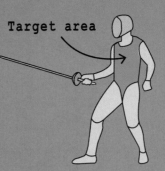

Target area

In foil, fencers score points by touching their opponent's chest with the tip of the sword.

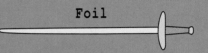

Foil

Épée

Target area

The épée is a slightly heavier weapon than the foil. Fencers score points by touching any part of their opponent's body with the tip.

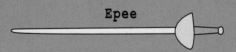

Epee

Sabre

Target area

In sabre, fencers score by hitting any part of their opponent's upper body except the hands with the tip or blade of the sword.

Sabre

Number of players: 2

Equipment: Sword and protective equipment

Tennis

Tennis is a racquet sport where players take turns to **hit a ball** over a net into the other side of the court.

Players have to master several types of shot, including the serve, volley, forehand, backhand, and lob.

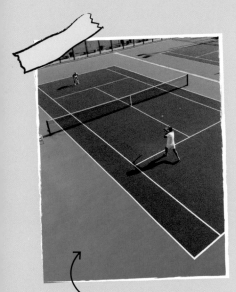

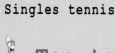
Singles tennis

Singles or doubles

Tennis can be played against one opponent (called "singles") or as a pair against two opponents (called "doubles"). Singles games use **part** of the court and doubles games use the **whole** court.

Doubles tennis

Top tournaments

The four biggest tournaments in tennis are known as the "**Grand Slams**" or majors. These are Wimbledon, the French Open, the US Open, and the Australian Open.

If a player serves and their opponent

FACT FILE

Type of sport: Racquet

3 GAMES | **1** SETS **0** | **2** GAMES

Game, Set, Match

Scoring in tennis can be a little tricky. Players win a **game** by scoring four points. However, if both players have scored three points, the game goes on until one player gains a lead of two points.

When a player wins six games, they win a **set**. But if the scores are tied at six games all, the players play a special game called a "tie-break".

Men play best of five sets and women play best of three. The overall winner wins the **match**.

The points are counted as "love" (0 points), 15 (1 point), 30 (2 points), and 40 (3 points). Nobody knows for sure how this system came about!

can't hit the ball, it's called an "ACE".

Number of players: 2-4

Equipment: Racquet and balls

Badminton

Badminton is a racquet sport where players hit a **shuttlecock** over a **net**. Singles matches are played between two people, and doubles between four.

Racquet

How to play

Players hit the shuttlecock over onto the other side of the net. Players then hit the shuttlecock back and forth until it **hits the ground**, the net, or goes out of the court.

Then and now

Although modern badminton came from Europe, it's most **popular in Asia**. It has been an Olympic sport since 1992, and Asian players have won by far the most medals.

FACT FILE

Type of sport:  Racquet

Shuttlecock

Strange-looking ball!

Shuttlecocks are made from overlapping feathers fixed to a cork base. They are usually plastic but can be made with **goose feathers**.

Honk!

China's Lin Dan is widely thought of as the best badminton player ever.

Badminton is the second most played sport in the world. It used to be called "battledore and shuttlecock".

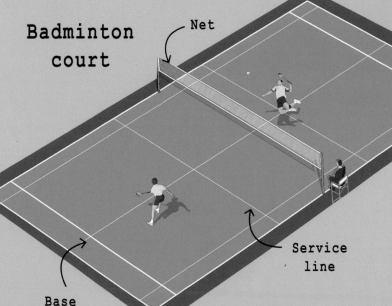

Badminton court

Net

Service line

Base line

Each player is only allowed to strike the shuttlecock once before it crosses the net.

Squash

Squash is a racquet sport played on a court with walls. It's one of the **fastest** and most intense sports to play.

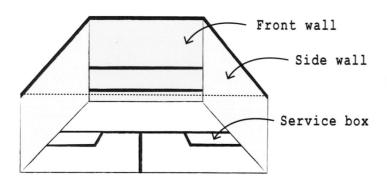

Front wall

Side wall

Service box

Aim of the game

Players serve from the service box, then take turns hitting the ball onto the **front wall** of the court. Players can **bounce** the ball off the side or back walls, just as long as it hits the front wall. The ball is only allowed to bounce on the ground **once**.

Scoring

Scoring systems vary, but usually the first player to win **11 points** wins the game (called a "set"). A match is usually made up of three or five sets.

Bouncing balls

Squash players choose their ball depending on their skill level. Each ball is marked by different coloured **dots**.

Blue balls are best for beginners. They are fast-paced and have a very high bounce.

Red balls are medium-paced with a high bounce. They are mostly used by medium-level players.

Yellow balls are slow with a low bounce, and are used by advanced players.

Double yellow balls are used by expert players. They are extra slow with a very low bounce.

FACT FILE   Type of sport:    Racquet

Squash is played by more than 25 million people. There are 50,000 squash courts in 185 countries.

Greatest ever

Pakistan's **Jahangir Khan** is the best player in the history of squash. He once won **556** competitive matches in a row, which is an all-time record for any professional sport!

Squash is a very good form of exercise because players use lots of energy when they play.

It's your serve, captain!

There was even a squash court on the *Titanic*!

Number of players: 2-4

Equipment: Squash racquet and ball

Table tennis

Also known as **"ping pong"**, table tennis is a lightning-quick racquet sport where players use a wooden paddle to hit a ball back and forth across a table.

How to play

Players hit the ball over a net in the middle of the table so it **bounces** on the other side. If a player's shot misses the table, hits the net, or they can't return their opponent's shot, the other player or team gets a point. Games are usually played to 11.

Origins

Table tennis was invented in England in the 1800s as an after-dinner game. Today, it's played all over the world, and is **China's national sport**.

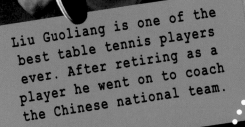

Liu Guoliang is one of the best table tennis players ever. After retiring as a player he went on to coach the Chinese national team.

FACT FILE

Type of sport: Racquet

Table tennis balls are small and light. Players need super-fast reflexes to return them in time.

Playing with paddles

Players hit the balls with small wooden paddles covered in rubber. One side is designed to add **spin** to the ball, and the other side to add no spin.

Top players hit the ball extremely fast.

China has been the most successful nation at the World Table Tennis Championships, winning 145 gold medals.

Table tennis is the world's most popular racquet sport.

Archery

Archery is the art of using a **bow** to shoot **arrows** at a **target**. The closer an archer gets their arrows to the centre of the target, the more points they score.

An ancient art

People have been using bows and arrows for thousands of years. They were originally used for **hunting**, then became a battle weapon before guns and cannons were invented.

During the Middle Ages, archers could shoot between 10–12 arrows a minute.

 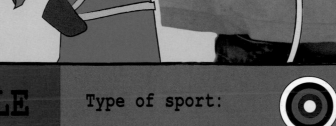

FACT FILE   Type of sport: Target

Olympic archery

Archery became an Olympic sport in **1900** but wasn't a permanent one until 1972. **South Korea** has been the most successful nation, picking up 23 gold medals over the years.

South Korea's Kim Soo-Nyung is the most successful archer in Olympic history. She has won four gold medals.

← Arrow

The type of bow used at the Olympics is called a "recurve bow". It's based on a design that is 3,500 years old!

← Arm guard

Recurve bow ↘

Hitting the target

Archers aim their arrows at a target with **ten rings**. Hitting the centre circle – the **"bullseye"** is worth **ten points**. Every ring further away from the bullseye is worth **one less point**.

Number of players:

Equipment

Bow and arrows

Darts

The first darts were arrows that had been cut down.

Darts is a sport where players score points by throwing small **arrows** called "darts" at a round **target**.

How to play

Players start with a score of 301 or 501 and try to reach **exactly zero**. They take turns throwing three darts, adding up the score, and subtracting it from their total. Players must finish on a "double" or the "inner-bullseye."

The board

A dartboard is a round target made of different sections numbered from one to 20. Each section also has a **double** and **triple** ring worth double or triple points, an **outer bullseye** (worth 25 points), and an **inner bullseye** (worth 50).

Quick maths

Darts players need to be accurate, but they also need to be good at **maths**. If they make a mistake, they need to quickly work out a new way to get to zero in the fewest throws possible.

England's Phil Taylor is the greatest darts player of all time. His nickname is "The Power".

FACT FILE

Type of sport:

Target

180!

The highest score a player can achieve in a single turn is 180. To do this they must throw all three darts into the triple 20 ring, which gives:

60 + 60 + 60 = 180!

Outer bullseye

Double

301−180=???

Inner bullseye

Triple

Extreme sports

These sports are for people who **live life on the edge**! They involve risk, speed, height, a battle against Mother Nature, or all of the above!

Parkour

Developed in France in the 1980s, parkour is also known as free-running. The aim is to move over and through obstacles by running, jumping, and climbing.

BMX

Cyclists on BMX bikes race around a dirt track with bumps, ramps, and sharp turns. BMX stands for "bicycle motocross".

White-water rafting

White-water rafters go down a river's fast-moving rapids on an inflatable raft.

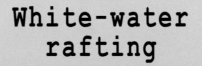

BASE jumping

BASE jumping is similar to skydiving, except people leap from high objects, such as buildings or cliffs, instead of out of a plane.

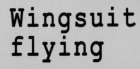

Skydiving

Skydivers leap out of a plane and then freefall before opening their parachutes to land gently on the ground.

Wingsuit flying

Wingsuit fliers jump out of a plane and use special winged suits to glide through the air before parachuting to the ground.

Parasailing

Parasailers are towed behind a fast boat, while strapped to a parasail, which lifts up and flies above the water.

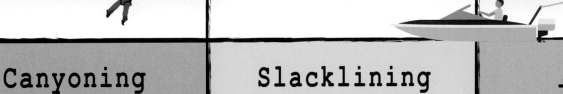

Canyoning

Canyoning is a way of exploring canyons by walking, scrambling, climbing, jumping, and swimming.

Slacklining

This is a sport where people walk on a rope between two points. The rope is usually high above the ground.

Bungee jumping

Bungee jumpers jump from a great height with an elastic rope fixed to their ankles which springs them back up.

Mountaineering

Mountaineering, or **alpinism,** is the name for climbing mountains, but it also involves other types of climbing, both indoor and out.

Race to the top

People have always climbed mountains, but in 1760, Swiss scientist and climber Horace-Bénédict de Saussure made news by offering a reward to anyone who could climb Mount Blanc in France. Then, in 1854, English mountaineer Sir Alfred Wills founded the first climbing club, helping start **the Golden Age of Alpinism.**

Clamps

Sir Alfred Wills

All the gear

Equipment varies based on **conditions**. In snow and ice, climbers wear **crampons** (a special spiked boot) and use an ice pick for **grip**. In rocky conditions, they hammer **clamps** into the rock, which they attach ropes to, and wear smooth shoes for grip.

Crampons

Ice pick

Dangers

Mountaineers face many dangers when climbing peaks, including **rock falls**, **ice falls**, **avalanches**, and **crevasses**. But a change in the **weather** is sometimes the greatest threat. At heights, weather can change quickly, leaving climbers stranded.

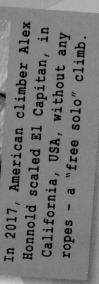
In 2017, American climber Alex Honnold scaled El Capitan, in California, USA, without any ropes – a "free solo" climb.

Climbers usually work in pairs and are roped together, with one "belaying" the other to catch them if they fall.

Type of sport: Extreme

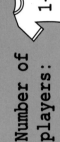

Number of players: 1+

Skateboarding

Skateboarders ride a **board with wheels** to do tricks and jumps. Skateboarding's first appearance at the Olympics was in Tokyo, Japan, in 2020.

The first skateboard competition was held in California, United States, in 1963.

Sidewalk surfing

Skateboarding was invented by American **surfers** who were looking for something fun to do when the **sea was calm**. They attached wheels to a short surfboard, and a new sport was born. It was originally called "sidewalk surfing".

Skateparks are areas specially built for skateboarders. The first was built in Arizona, USA, in 1965.

Type of sport: Extreme

Tricky!

There are lots of tricks to learn, but the "**ollie**" is the most important. This is where the rider and board leap into the air. It is one of the first tricks a skateboarder must master.

The "ollie" was created by American skateboarder Alan "Ollie" Gelfand in 1978.

Before skateparks were invented, skateboarders used to practise in empty SWIMMING POOLS!

America's Tony Hawk is the most successful skateboarder in history. He is famous for a trick called the "900", which is two-and-a-half full turns in the air.

 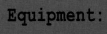

Snooker

Snooker is played on a big table, with a stick called a **cue**, and a set of balls. The aim is to knock the "cue ball" into other balls so they fall into the table's pockets.

Potting

Knocking the balls into the pockets is called **"potting"** them. Each coloured ball earns a different number of points when potted.

Pocket

Red (1)

Yellow (2)

Green (3)

Brown (4)

Blue (5)

Pink (6)

Black (7)

Early snooker balls were made from animal bones or tusks.

The balls must be potted in a special order: a red, then a colour, then a red, then a colour. The coloured balls are replaced each time until all 15 red balls are potted.

When all 15 red balls have been potted, the player pots the yellow, green, brown, blue, pink, and black balls in order.

Players keep going until they miss a pot. The winner is the player with the most points at the end of the game.

FACT FILE   Type of sport: Stick and ball

Players add chalk to the tip of their cue to help add spin to their shots.

Cue ball

Pool

Pool is a similar sport played on a smaller table with fewer balls. There are different versions, but in most, players pot their balls in any order, then end with the black.

Big break

Potting multiple balls in a row is called a **break**. A maximum break happens if a player pots all 15 red balls, followed by 15 blacks, and then all the other colours. This gives them a total score of **147**.

The word "snooker" comes from the word for an inexperienced soldier.

Number of players: 2

Equipment: Cue, balls, table

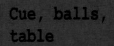

Bowling

Rolling a ball is simple, but bowling is much harder! There are two main types of bowling: **lawn bowls** and **ten-pin**.

Lawn bowls

The aim of lawn bowls is to roll a ball so it stops as close as possible to a smaller ball called a **"jack"**. It's played on grass.

Bowl

The balls used in lawn bowls are not perfectly round. This means skilled players can curve the ball when they bowl it.

Jack

Similar versions of **LAWN BOWLS** called **BOULES**, **RAFFA**,

Ten-pin

In ten-pin bowling, a player bowls a ball down a **wooden lane**. The aim is to knock down as many of the ten pins as possible.

Bowling ball

Gutters

FACT FILE   Type of sport:    Ball

Long ago in England, bowls was banned because the King thought it would distract soldiers from practising their archery!

Scoring

The player whose ball is closest to the jack when all balls have been played **wins a point**. If a player has two balls closest, they get two points. The first player to reach 21 points wins.

BOCCE, and **PÉTANQUE** are played around the world.

If a player knocks down all ten pins in one attempt, it's called a "strike".

Three strikes in a row are called a "TURKEY!"

How to play

Bowlers have two attempts to knock down all ten pins. The bowling lane has "gutters" down each side that collect badly bowled balls.

Pins →

Ten-pin bowling is the most played sport in the USA.

Number of players: 2–6

Equipment: 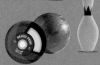 Bowls and jack or bowling ball and pins

Golf

Golf is a sport where players use clubs to hit a ball into a hole. The aim is to get around a golf course in the **fewest** number of shots.

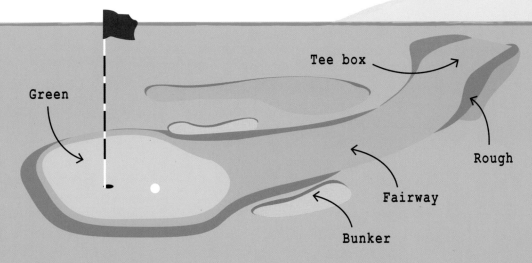

Green

Tee box

Rough

Fairway

Bunker

The course

A golf course is usually made of 9 or 18 holes. For each hole, the player starts on a **tee box**, hits the ball down the **fairway**, trying to avoid the **rough** (long grass) and **bunkers** (sand traps). Once they are on the **green**, the player tries to putt the ball into the **hole**.

Astronauts have even played golf on the MOON!

Wood

Iron

Putter

Types of club

Golfers use different types of clubs for different shots. **Woods** help players hit the ball a long way, **irons** are used for more precise shots, and a **putter** is used to tap the ball into the hole.

Every hole has a "par" number, which is the number of shots you are expected to take to get the ball in the hole. The more shots under par you get, the better.

-4	Condor	Four shots better than par
-3	Albatross (Double Eagle)	Three shots better than par
-2	Eagle	Two shots better than par
-1	Birdie	One shot better than par
0	Par	The expected number of shots
+1	Bogey	One shot worse than par
+2	Double bogey	Two shots worse than par
+3	Triple bogey	Three shots worse than par

The first golf balls were stuffed with goose feathers and were known as "featheries".

Get crazy!

Crazy golf is a fun version of golf played on a tiny course using only a putter. Players have to avoid obstacles and make trick shots.

Windmill obstacle

Number of players: 1-4

Equipment: Golf clubs and golf ball

Unusual sports

Some sports around the world sound too weird or silly to be true but, believe it or not, these are real sports...

Chess boxing

Chess boxing is exactly what it sounds like — rounds of chess and rounds of boxing! Players win by getting checkmate in chess or knocking out an opponent in boxing.

Extreme ironing

The aim is to iron clothes in extreme conditions, such as while skydiving, underwater, or in a snowstorm!

Toe wrestling

Toe wrestling is a little like arm wrestling. Competitors lock big toes and try to pin down their opponent's foot.

Cheese rolling

Players chase a wheel of cheese down a hill and try to catch up with it. Usually they just fall over though!

Shin kicking

Two opponents line up against each other, grab each other by the collar, and actually kick each other in the shin!

Octopush

Also called underwater hockey, players move a puck across the bottom of a pool into their opponent's goal.

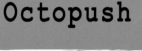

Bog snorkelling

Competitors try to swim two lengths of a muddy ditch as fast as possible.

Egg throwing

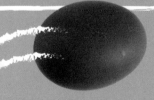

The aim in egg throwing is to throw and catch eggs from the furthest distance possible without breaking them. It's harder than it sounds!

Fjerljeppen

This sport comes from the Netherlands. It means "far leaping". People shimmy up a pole as it is falling and try to land on the other side of a canal.

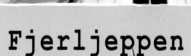

Ice hockey

Sliding
sports

Ski jumping

Biathlon

Figure
skating

Skiing

Winter sports

When summer is over, there are lots of sports to play on the **ice and snow**. All of these sports are part of the Winter Olympics, which happens every four years. Wrap up warm and take a look at these chilly sports.

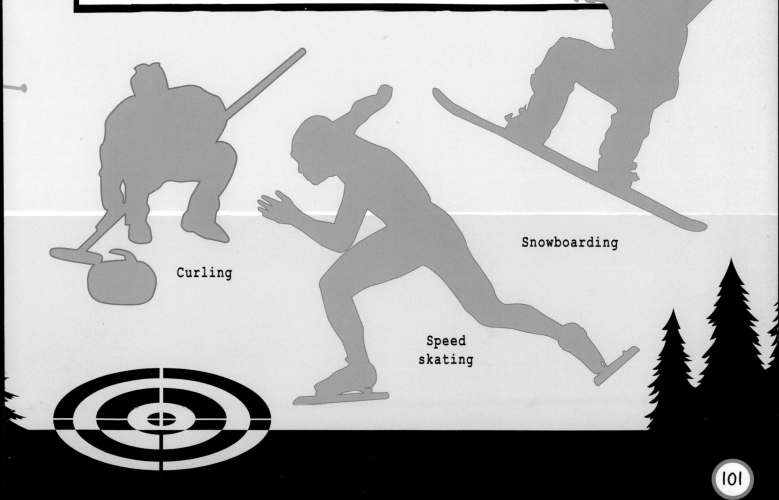

Curling

Speed skating

Snowboarding

Skiing

Skiers have been gliding over snow for fun, and to get around, for thousands of years. Skiing became popular as a sport in the 18th century, and there are now two types: **alpine** and **Nordic**.

Alpine

In alpine skiing, skiers glide **down hills**. There are **four events**: downhill, slalom, giant slalom, and super giant slalom (Super G).

Downhill is all about speed. Skiers start near the top of a mountain and rush down a steep, twisty course as quickly as possible.

Slalom is a shorter race for master turners. Skiers make short, quick turns between poles or gates.

Giant slalom skiers race over a longer course between a series of gates. The gates are spaced further apart than in slalom races.

Super G combines the speed of downhill with the precision skiing of giant slalom.

Downhill skiers reach speeds of up to 130KPH (81MPH).

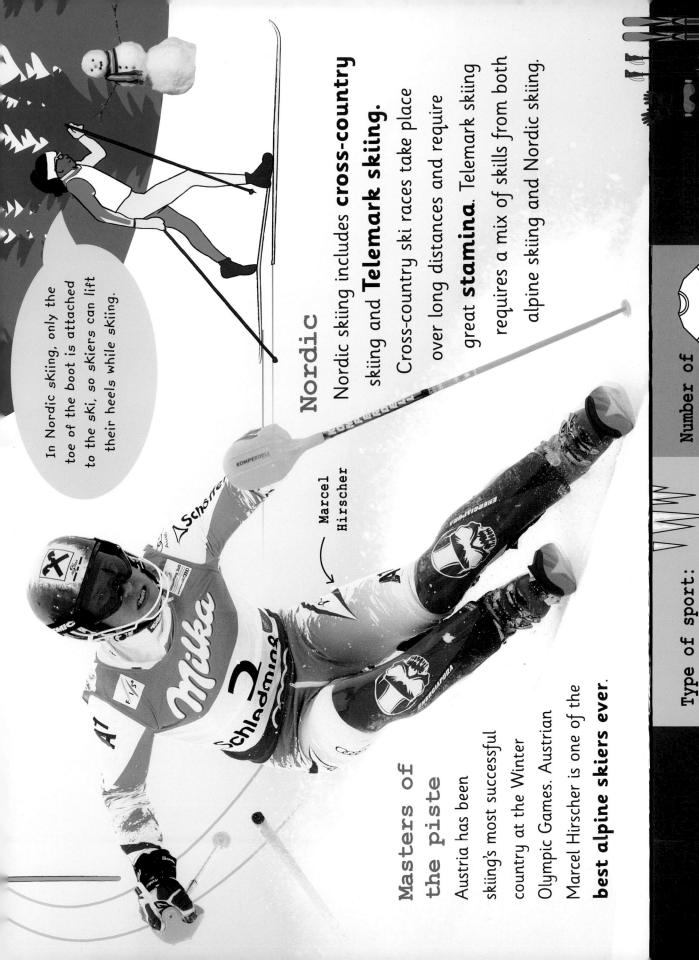

In Nordic skiing, only the toe of the boot is attached to the ski, so skiers can lift their heels while skiing.

Nordic

Nordic skiing includes **cross-country skiing and Telemark skiing.** Cross-country ski races take place over long distances and require great **stamina**. Telemark skiing requires a mix of skills from both alpine skiing and Nordic skiing.

Marcel Hirscher

Masters of the piste

Austria has been skiing's most successful country at the Winter Olympic Games. Austrian Marcel Hirscher is one of the **best alpine skiers ever**.

Type of sport: Winter

Number of players: 1

Ski jumping

Ski jumping is a sport where skiers speed down a ramp, launch through the air, and try to jump as **far as they can**.

Ski jumpers can reach speeds of **105KPH (65mph)** on the biggest hills.

Taking flight

When ski jumpers launch from the ramp, they can glide through the air for around 10 seconds and travel as far as **two football pitches**!

Jumping ramp

Take-off table

Ski jumping started in Norway more than 100 years ago.

Sondre Norheim came up with the idea to fully strap his boots to skis rather than just the toe. He used his invention to win the first-ever ski jumping competition in Høydalsmo, Norway, in 1866.

FACT FILE

High on the hill

Ski jumping venues are called **hills**. Hills are made up of a **jumping ramp**, a **take-off table**, and a **landing hill**.

Ski jumpers hold their skis in a V-shape when flying through the air to help them jump further.

Ski jumping has been an Olympic sport since 1924.

Austrian Stefan Kraft holds the world record for the longest ski jump at 253.5m (832ft)

Landing hill

Number of players: 1

Equipment: Skis, boots, helmet, goggles, gloves

Biathlon

Biathlon is a winter endurance sport that combines cross-country **skiing** and rifle **shooting**. The biathlete who records the fastest time wins.

Shooting

Ski and shoot

Competitors ski around the track as quickly as possible, stopping at several spots to shoot at **targets**. If they miss, they must ski around a penalty loop, or have a minute added to their time.

Biathlon means "two contests".

FACT FILE

King of Biathlon

Norway's Ole Einar Bjørndalen is one of the **greatest** biathletes ever. Ole won 13 medals at the Winter Olympics, 8 of them gold.

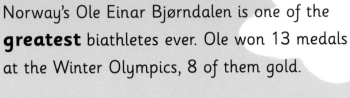

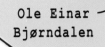

Ole Einar Bjørndalen

Cross-country skiing

Target

Biathletes carry their rifles on their backs as they ski.

Superhuman shooting

Shooting a rifle always takes skill, but it's especially tricky during a biathlon. Cross-country skiing is tiring, so when an athletes stops to shoot, their heart is pounding, making it very hard to hold a rifle steady.

Biathlon goes back 2,000 years, when Scandinavian hunters set off skiing with a weapon over their shoulder.

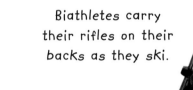

Snowboarding

The sport of snowboarding was inspired by **skateboarding**, **surfing**, and **skiing**. A snowboarder glides down slopes on a long board.

Snowboard styles

From **racing** and performing **tricks**, to **jumping** as high as possible, there are lots of ways for boarders to enjoy the snow.

Slopestyle

Snowboarders perform tricks while riding down a course packed with obstacles such as jumps, boxes, or rails.

Jibbing

This is a technique where a boarder rides and performs tricks on surfaces such as rails, benches, logs, and rocks.

Racing

Snowboarders race down a course similar to a giant slalom course used in skiing. Riders have to pass through a series of gates.

Big air

Riders perform tricks after launching themselves off a big ramp.

Freeriding

This is snowboarding on an open mountainside. There is no set course or rules to follow.

Snowboarding became a Winter Olympic sport at the 1998 Games in Nagano, Japan.

Snurfing

Although it developed in several places, the origins of snowboarding go back to 1965, when American engineer **Sherman Poppen** strapped two skis together so his daughters could have more control while skiing. He called the invention a **"snurfer"** and the idea caught on!

Half-pipe

Boardercross

Several riders race down a special course. The first to cross the finishing line wins the race.

Alpine snowboarding

This is when snowboarders ride on the runs used by skiers. It's fast and full of skilful turns.

Half-pipe

Riders perform tricks while riding along a huge, semi-circular tube.

Number of players: 1

Equipment: Snowboard, helmet, goggles, gloves

Speed skating

There are two types of speed skating: long track and short track. Both have the same goal — race around an ice track as **fast as possible**!

Short track racing was invented in the USA because there were plenty of ice rinks.

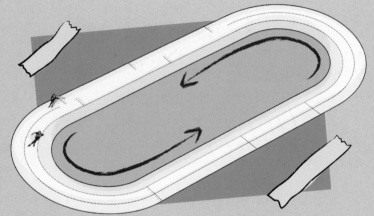

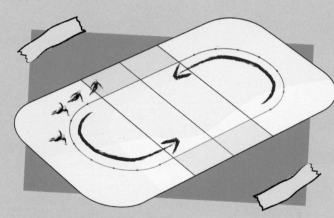

Long track races are held on a large oval. Only two skaters race at one time. Races can be between 500m and 10000m. The first to finish is the winner.

Short track races take place on ice rinks. The skaters all race at once but must not get in each others' way and are disqualified if they do. Races are between 500m and 5000m.

Speed skaters look like they glide effortlessly on the ice, but they're moving at fast speeds!

South Korean flag

Korean dominance

Since short track speed skating became an Olympic event in 1992, **South Korean** skaters have dominated, winning 48 medals, including 24 golds.

With a record 11 Olympic medals, Ireen Wüst of the Netherlands is the most successful long track speed skater ever.

Ireen Wüst

Steady skating

Like all sports, winning can sometimes be a matter of **luck**! In the 2002 Olympics, Australia's Steven Bradbury was in last place, but all of his opponents fell over. He stayed on his skates, crossed the finish line first, and won gold.

Steven Bradbury

Skaters always race in an ANTI-CLOCKWISE direction.

Ice skates

Figure skating

Figure skating is a sport where individuals or pairs perform rehearsed **dance routines** on ice while wearing **skates**.

Skating's start

The sport of figure skating is credited to Americans **Edward Bushell**, who introduced the boots that allowed skaters to jump and turn, and **Jackson Haines**, a ballet master who added dance elements.

Jackson Haines

Routines

Skaters perform **dances** called **programmes**, which must include spins, jumps, and throws (if dancing in pairs). Judges award marks based on how difficult the routine is.

FACT FILE

Type of sport: Winter

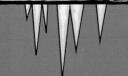

Ice skating existed long before the sport. As early as the 13th century, the Dutch used ice skates to travel around on frozen canals.

The triple axel is one of the most difficult jumps.

Jumps

Skaters perform jumps with different names such as the **toe loop**, **trip**, **lutz**, **salchow**, and **axel**. Skaters use diffferent parts of the blade on their skates to perform these jumps.

Sonja Henie

Figure skating has produced some world-famous stars such as Norway's Sonja Henie. She made her Olympic debut at 11 years old, and later became a Hollywood film star.

Figure skaters must be strong, agile, and ACROBATIC.

Number of players: 1-2

Equipment: 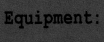 Ice skates

Ice hockey

Ice hockey is similar to field hockey, but instead of being played on grass, it's played on **ice** with **skates** strapped on.

Out on the rink

Ice hockey players wear skates and move around an ice court called a **"rink"**. Instead of a ball, they hit a small disc called a **puck**.

Staying safe

With sharp skates, flying pucks, big sticks, and fast, strong players whizzing around, players need to wear **pads**. The **goalkeeper** has the most dangerous job, so is covered head to toe in **protective clothing**.

Puck

FACT FILE   Type of sport: Winter

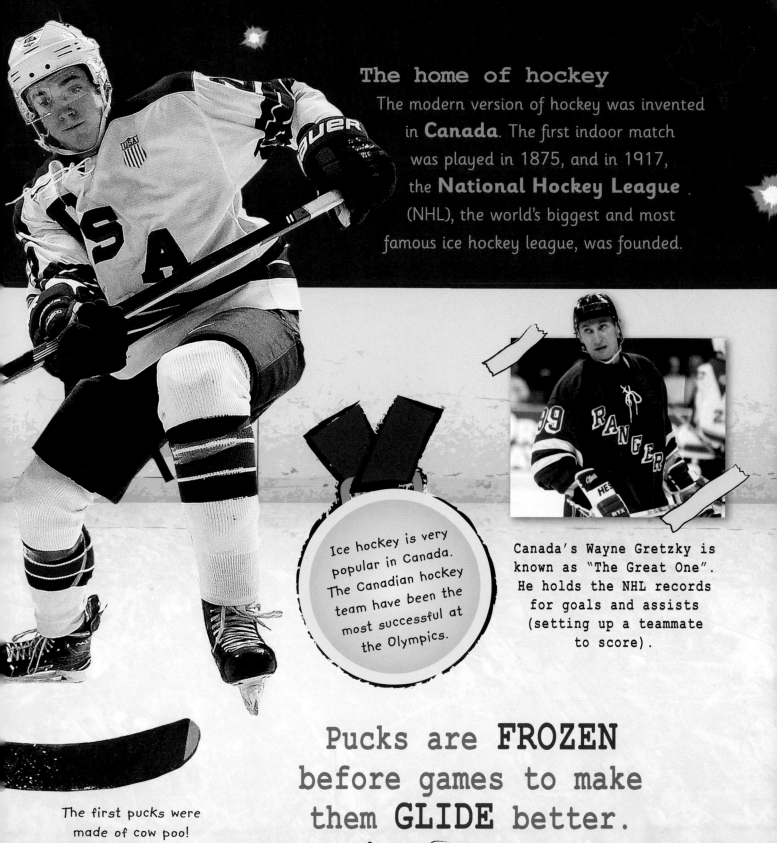

The home of hockey

The modern version of hockey was invented in **Canada**. The first indoor match was played in 1875, and in 1917, the **National Hockey League** (NHL), the world's biggest and most famous ice hockey league, was founded.

Ice hockey is very popular in Canada. The Canadian hockey team have been the most successful at the Olympics.

Canada's Wayne Gretzky is known as "The Great One". He holds the NHL records for goals and assists (setting up a teammate to score).

Pucks are FROZEN before games to make them GLIDE better.

The first pucks were made of cow poo!

Players per team: 6

Equipment:

Puck, skates, helmet, hockey stick and pads

Sliding sports

Sliding sports are winter sports where people slide over **ice** with **sleds**. Some sliding sports are high-speed time trials on a **special track**, while others are long-distance races over frozen land.

> Bobsleigh gets its name from the way riders bob back and forth in the sled to make it go faster.

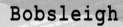
Bobsleigh

Bobsleigh

Bobsleigh is a winter sport where teams of **two** or **four** riders speed down a **twisty track**. The aim is to go as fast as possible!

> Bobsleigh tracks are made of concrete, then coated with ice. There are only 16 tracks in the world used for competitions.

Luge

In the luge, riders **lie on their backs** on a sled and slide **feet first** around a bobsleigh track. Like bobsleigh, the aim is to record the fastest time possible.

Germany have dominated the luge at the Winter Olympics.

Skeleton

Luge

Skeleton

Skeleton is a high-speed sliding sport in which riders race **head-first** down a bobsleigh track. They lie on their **front** on a small sled.

Skeleton riders can reach speeds of 130kph (80mph)!

Sled dog racing

This sport is particularly popular in the world's **Arctic regions** – Russia, Greenland, and North America. A team of **dogs** pulls a **sled** and **rider** (musher). Teams race over courses, and the fastest team wins.

Curling

In curling, teams slide big **stones** along a slippery sheet of ice, and try to get them to stop on a target called the **house**. The closer they get to the middle of the house, the better.

Players can use their stone to knock the other team's stones away from the target to stop them getting points.

Curling stone

House

At the Olympics

Curling was first played at the Winter Olympics at Calgary, Canada, in 1998. **Canada** have been the most successful nation, winning three golds in the men's event and two golds in the women's event.

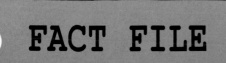

Skilful sliding

Sliding the stone to exactly where you want can be tricky on the smooth ice. To help it along, **"sweepers"** brush the ice in front of the stone with special brooms. The harder they sweep, the further the stone travels.

Sweeper

The captain of a curling team is called the "SKIP".

The skip shouts out orders to the rest of the team so that they know where and how hard to sweep the ice with their brooms.

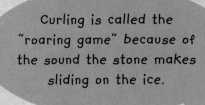

Curling is called the "roaring game" because of the sound the stone makes sliding on the ice.

A very old game

Curling has been played in Scotland, Belgium, and the Netherlands for centuries. The oldest curling stone ever found dates to 1511. It was found in a pond in Scotland.

Players per team: 4

Equipment: 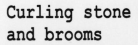 Curling stone and brooms

Diving

Kayaking

Water polo

Swimming

Rowing

Water sports

While most sports are played on land, there are plenty that take place on or in the water. Whether they involve swimming or steering a boat, all these sports require **speed**, **power**, **and stamina**. Let's dive in!

Sailing

Surfing

Swimming

Swimmers use their arms and legs to push themselves through water. There are four different swimming **strokes**, each with its own technique.

Top swimmers are very muscular and usually have broad shoulders.

Freestyle

Also known as front crawl, this is the fastest stroke. The swimmer moves their arms forward in turns while constantly kicking their feet.

Butterfly

This is the most difficult stroke. The swimmer throws both arms forwards then pulls them back along each side of their body, while performing a dolphin kick with their legs.

Swimming is one of only five sports that have been at every Olympic Games.

Open-water swimming

Swimming in **lakes** or in the **sea** is known as open-water swimming. Open-water swimming is a long race that requires amazing stamina.

Freedivers hold their breath and try to dive as deep as possible. Top freedivers can hold their breath for up to ten minutes!

The first Olympic swimming competition was held in the sea.

10

Backstroke

The swimmer lies on their back and kicks their legs while lifting one arm over their head and then pulling it through the water. They then repeat with the other arm.

Breaststroke

This is the slowest stroke. The swimmer pushes both arms straight out in front of them, then pulls each arm to their side in a big semi circle. The legs perform a "frog kick".

Number of players: 1-8

Equipment: Swiming costume, goggles, cap

Diving

Diving is the skill of **jumping** into water from a height while performing acrobatic moves.

Types of diving

There are two forms of competitive diving: **platform diving**, which takes place in a pool, and **cliff diving**, where divers leap from a platform into the sea.

Cliff diving

In cliff diving, divers **launch** themselves from a cliff into the sea. No one knows the exact origins, but it's been done for hundreds of years in many parts of the world.

Platform diving

Divers, either **alone** or in **pairs**, leap from platforms into a pool. During the dive they perform **moves** and are judged on how difficult the dive is and how well they pulled it off.

Diving partners Guo Jingjing and Wu Minxia from China are two of the best divers ever.

Guo Jingjing

There are cliff diving tournaments all over the world.

If a diver enters the water without making a splash, it is known as a "RIP".

Wu Minxia →

Divers must get into one of these four **positions** during a dive:

Straight: a diver is not allowed to have any bend in the hips or knees.

Pike: a diver bends their body but keeps their legs straight.

Free: a twisted dive that includes a combination of the other three dives.

Tuck: a diver tucks their body into a ball.

Surfing

Surfers, sometimes called "wave riders", stand on surfboards to **catch a wave** and ride it back to shore.

Many surfers have BOLD, personal designs on their boards.

Hawaii

The rise of surfing

Surfing has been part of the culture of the Pacific Islands for centuries. Pacific Islanders shared surfing with the world by **teaching tourists** how to catch waves.

Experienced surfers can do tricks as they ride the wave.

To ride a wave, surfers lie on their boards and face the shore. When a good wave comes, they paddle and try to match its speed. Once the wave carries them forwards, they stand up and ride it.

FACT FILE   Type of sport:    Water

Through the tube

When a surfer rides inside the curl of a breaking wave, it's called a **"tube ride"**.

Tube riders try to stand inside the curl without it collapsing on them.

When a surfer comes off their board, it's called a "WIPEOUT".

George Freeth © 1914 - 2014

Hawaiian lifeguard George Freeth is considered one of the fathers of surfing. Raised on the beaches of Hawaii, Freeth was spotted surfing and invited to California to show off his skills and love of surfing.

Water polo

This sport is a little like handball or rugby, but in water. Two teams **swim around**, passing a ball to each other, and shooting at the other team's goal.

Start of a sport

In 1877, Scottish swimming instructor William Wilson came up with a set of rules, and the first water polo match took place on the River Dee in **Scotland**. After that the sport became popular in the UK and around the world.

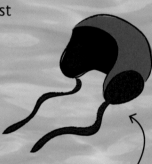

Ear guards are used for protection, but also help identify who is on each team.

Ear guards

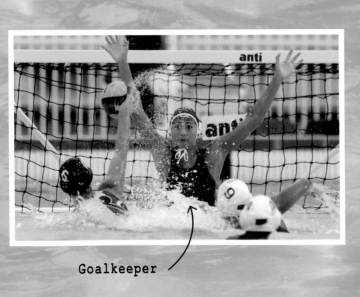

Goalkeeper

Playing the game

Unlike in most team sports, water polo players don't really stay in any set **positions** (other than the goalkeeper). The other players can move around the pool depending on the situation.

FACT FILE

Players can only hold the ball in ONE HAND.

Contact sport

Players are allowed to grab each others' arms and legs, but most games are very clean. However, the 1956 Olympic game between Hungary and the USSR was **so rough** that players got injured and it became known as the "Blood in the Water" match. The countries were at war at the time.

Players use a technique known as an "egg beater kick" to stay upright as they play. It's called this because the motion of the player's legs is like the motion cooks make when they whisk eggs.

Egg beater kick

Players per team:	7	Equipment:		Swimwear, mouth guard, ear guards, ball

Kayaking

Kayaking is a water sport where people move a **small boat** through water using a special paddle.

Kayaking can be slow and relaxing in calm waters, or exhilarating in dangerously fast rapids.

The LONGER a kayak is...

Ancient transport

Kayaks were invented by the Inuit people from North America. They were originally used for hunting and fishing. The word kayak means **"hunter's boat"**.

FACT FILE

Type of sport: Water

White-water kayaking

In 1931, Germany's Adolf Anderle kayaked down the **rushing waters** of the Salzachöfen Gorge in Austria. This is thought to be the birth of white-water kayaking, which gets its name because rushing water rapids look white.

In 1928, Germany's Franz Romer kayaked across the Atlantic Ocean. It took him 58 days!

...the FASTER it goes.

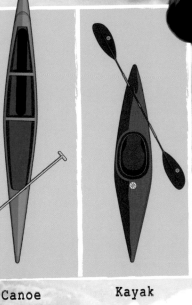

Canoe   Kayak

Kayak or canoe?

A lot of people mix up kayaks with canoes, but a good way to tell the difference is to remember kayakers sit **inside the boat**, and canoes have a raised seat. They also use different paddles.

Rowing

Rowers use **oars** to move their **boat** through water. They race each other one-on-one, or in teams of up to eight rowers and a **cox**, who steers and coordinates the other members of the team.

Up the river

Rowing has been a good way to move on water since ancient times. For centuries, ferrymen in London, England, took passengers up and down the **River Thames**, and eventually started racing to see who was fastest.

Every year since 1829, rowers from Oxford and Cambridge Universities row against each other in a famous race.

FACT FILE   Type of sport:    Water

At the first ever modern Olympics in 1896, the rowing competition had to be cancelled due to stormy weather!

British rower Steve Redgrave won gold at every Olympic Games between 1984 and 2000.

Cox

Rowers face backwards so they can pull their oars and move the boat. This means they can't see where they're going. Only the cox faces forwards.

Number of players: 1-9

Equipment: Rowing boat, oars

Sailing

Sailing boats use the power of the **wind** to move over **water**.

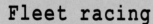

Sailing is one of the world's oldest forms of transport, but it's also a popular sport.

Buoy

Sailing as a sport

There are lots of **different types** of sailing **races**, but the boats in each one are usually a similar size and type. The amount of people sailing a boat (the crew) can be as little as one, or up to 15.

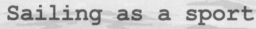

Fleet racing

Boats receive points for where they finish in a race. The winner is the boat with the best score after all the races are finished.

Match racing

Two boats race against each other, and the first boat to cross the finish line wins. The world's most famous sailing race, the America's Cup, is a match race.

Team racing

This is a tactical race in which a team of three boats takes on another team of three boats. The team with the best overall score wins the race.

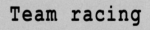

FACT FILE

Sails

Boom

Laura Dekker from the Netherlands sailed around the world by herself when she just age 16.

Speed sailing

In *speed sailing*, boats compete individually and try to go as fast as possible.

Rudder

Bits of a boat

There are lots of differet types of boat, and they can look very different to each other. But they all have **sails**, to catch the wind, a **boom**, to help control the angle of the sails, and a **rudder**, to help steer.

Number of players:

1–15

Equipment:

Boat, life vest

Water sports

Water sports are activities that take place either **in the water**, or **on the water**.

Scuba-diving

With an oxygen tank, scuba-divers can swim underwater without needing to come up for air.

ON THE WATER

Water-skiing

Water-skiers stand on skis and hold a cable attached to a speed boat. The boat drags the skier across the water.

Jet-skiing

Riders stand on a motorized jet ski and power their way across the water. Some jet-skiers race against each other.

Kite-surfing

Kite-surfers stand on a board and use a kite to pull them across the surface of the water.

IN THE WATER

Snorkelling

Snorkellers use a mask and a pipe called a snorkel to help them breathe while their faces are underwater.

Synchronized swimming

Swimmers perform rehearsed moves together in a pool. The aim is to do the same move at the exact same time.

Wakeboarding

This is similar to water-skiing, but wakeboarders use a board instead of skis.

Wind-surfing

Wind-surfers ride a board that has a sail attached to it. The power of the wind moves them through the water.

Dragonboat racing

A team of paddlers move a long, canoe-like boat through the water, often racing against other boats. Teams can be as large as 20 paddlers.

Go

Playground
games

Dodgeball

Tug of war

Games

What's more fun than a game? Some are so simple they can be played by anyone with no special equipment. Some require strength, some require agility, and then there are board games that require brains and planning. Which is your **favourite**?

Ultimate

Chess

Ancient games

People have been playing board games for a long, long time. Some of these ancient games are around **5,000 years old**!

Latrunculi

Also known as Mercenaries, this Roman strategy game was played on a board with a grid similar to chess or checkers.

Mehen

No one knows how this ancient Egyptian board game was played, but the board itself was shaped like a snake!

→ Mehen board

Mancala

Mancala is still played today, but some people think a version of it was played in ancient Egyptian times.

Patolli

This game was popular in the Aztec Empire. Players threw stones or beans to decide how their pieces would move around a cross-shaped board.

Patolli ➜

Petteia

The ancient Greek game of petteia (robbers) was a little like the modern game of checkers. The aim is to capture all of your opponent's pieces.

Senet

This ancient Egyptian board game dates to around 3,100BCE! The word senet means "the game of pulling", but no one knows exactly how it was played.

Terni Lapilli

This game, played in the Roman Empire, was similar to the modern-day game of noughts and crosses (tic-tac-toe).

The Royal Game of Ur

This strategy game is also known as "The Game of 20 Squares". It was first played around 3,000BCE in Mesopotamia (ancient Iraq).

Playground games

Playing games is a **fun** way to make friends, but on top of that, games can teach you important skills such as **teamwork** and **coordination**.

Catch the dragon's tail

In this Chinese game, players line up with their hands on the shoulders of the person in front. The first person is the dragon's head and the person at the back is the tail. The "head" tries to catch the "tail" while the players in the middle stiffen and try to stop them.

Dan chhae jul normgi

In this traditional Korean game, two players turn a skipping rope while other players take turns trying to jump on the rope and stop it moving. If they succeed they become a rope holder, but if the rope catches their leg, they are out. The winner is the last player left.

Hide and seek

The rules of hide and seek are simple. The seeker covers their eyes and counts while everyone else hides. Then the seeker has to find them. The last person to be found is the winner.

Rock, paper, scissors

Two players count to three then use their hands to make the shape of either a rock (a fist), a piece of paper (a flat hand), or a pair of scissors (a V-shape). Rock beats scissors; paper beats rock; and scissors beats paper.

Forty forty

One player is "it" and must guard a "base", such as a tree. The other players run off and hide, then have to get back to the base without being tagged by the guard.

Ten ten

Ten ten is a popular clapping game from Nigeria where children face each other and clap their hands and move their legs to a rhythm.

Red rover

Two teams line up opposite each other and form chains by holding hands. The first team calls out: "Red rover, red rover, send (player's name) over." The player who has been called must leave their line, run to the other team, and try to break through the chain. If they do, they take a player to their team. If not, they join their opponents in the chain. By the end, one team has all the players.

143

More playground games

Here are some other playground games you can try. Some of these games are played **all around the world**, but will have different names.

It/Tag	Cat's cradle	Leap frog
This is the simplest of playground games. One person is "it" and must try to tag another player. If they tag another person, that person becomes the new "it", and the game continues.	This ancient game involves two or more players and a piece of string. Players twist the string into a special shape with their fingers and take turns making shapes with the string.	One player bends over or crouches while another vaults over them. That player then bend over and lets the other player vault over them.

YOU'RE "IT"

Double dutch

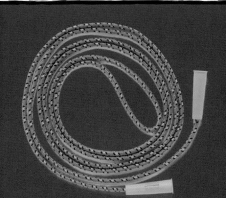

This is a skipping game that uses two long skipping ropes. The ropes are spun in opposite directions while two or more players jump in the middle.

Duck, duck, goose

All players sit in a circle, except one, who walks around the circle, tapping people's heads and saying whether they are a "duck" or a "goose". If someone is a goose, they have to get up and try to tag the person who tagged them before they can sit down in the goose's spot. If the goose can't do this, they become the person outside the circle.

Statues

This game is popular in Greece. Someone is chosen to be "it", closes their eyes and shouts "agalmata!" (which means "statue" in Greek). The other players have to freeze in the shape of famous statues and try not to move.

Capture the flag

Two teams place a flag in a special "base". The goal is to try to steal the other team's flag and return it to your base while also protecting your own flag and avoiding being tagged. If players are tagged they are stuck in "jail" and have to remain still until they are freed by one of their teammates.

Kongki noli

A traditional Korean game, Kongki noli involves players scattering five stones on the ground, throwing one into the air while picking up another. With each new round of the game, the player has to pick up more and more stones at once.

Tug of war

Tug of War was part of the Olympics between 1900 and 1920, but has not been included since.

Also known as rope-pulling, tug of war is a **test of strength**. Two teams pull on opposite ends of a rope to try to drag the other team to their side of a line.

Ancient origins

No one really knows where tug of war originated, but it's definitely **very old**. Ancient Chinese commanders used the sport to train soldiers, and it's likely generals in ancient Greece did the same.

FACT FILE   Type of sport: Team

The phrase TUG OF WAR was first used to describe battles. It wasn't a name for this game until much later.

The middle of the rope is marked to show when one team has successfully pulled the other to their side.

A Tug of war rope needs to be thick so it doesn't SNAP!

Centre line

Ultimate

In the game of ultimate, players throw a **flying disc** to their teammates while the other team tries to get it from them.

Ultimate origins

Ultimate was invented by a group of American **school children** in 1968. The sport's first proper rules were decided in 1970 and it has grown ever since.

Catching the disc by clapping your hands together is called a PANCAKE!

A popular brand of flying disc gets its name from a tin used to hold pies made by the Frisbie Pie Company.

FACT FILE   Type of sport: Throwing

Basic rules

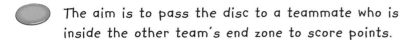 The game is played on a field similar to an American football pitch with an area called an end zone at each end.

The aim is to pass the disc to a teammate who is inside the other team's end zone to score points.

Players can pass the disc in any direction, but are not allowed to run with it. If an opponent catches a thrown disc, their team gets to keep it.

If the disc doesn't reach a teammate, is dropped, or goes out of the field of play, the other team gets it.

Players are not allowed to bump into or tackle each other.

Spirit of the game

Ultimate is one of very few team sports that does not use a **referee**. Instead, the players make all the decisions. This is because everyone who plays is expected to follow the "spirit of the game" and play fairly.

Rock, paper, scissors is sometimes used instead of a coin toss to decide which team starts the game with the disc.

Dodgeball

Dodgeball is a **fun** team sport where players try to hit their opponents with a ball, while avoiding being hit by balls **thrown** at them by opponents.

How to play

Two teams of six try to get as many of the other team's players out as they can.

- Players throw balls at the other team. If the ball hits an opponent, they are out; but, if they catch the ball, the player who threw it is out.

- Players can save a teammate if they catch the ball that hit them before it touches the ground.

- Players are only allowed to hold the ball for five seconds. If they hold it for longer, they have to give it to the other team.

- If a player steps outside the court or crosses into the other team's half, they are out.

- Games usually last for three minutes. The team with the most players left wins.

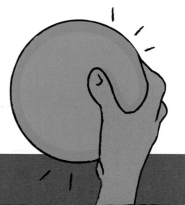

FACT FILE

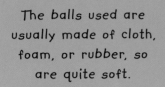
The balls used are usually made of cloth, foam, or rubber, so are quite soft.

Players are NOT allowed to aim at an opponent's HEAD.

Dangerous game

The sport is believed to have come from an African game from 200 years ago. Players **threw rocks at each other** to improve **hunting skills** and learn to work as a team.

Players per team: 6

Equipment:  Balls

Chess

Chess is a hugely popular **strategy** game that gets your brain planning moves and thinking ahead. It is played on a chequered board with 64 squares.

Rooks can travel any distance in a straight line.

Pawn　　　**Rook**　　　**Knight**

How to win

Each player has **16 pieces**: one king, one queen, two bishops, two knights, two rooks (castles), and eight pawns. The aim is to take your opponent's pieces and **checkmate** your opponent's king by trapping it where it can't move without being taken.

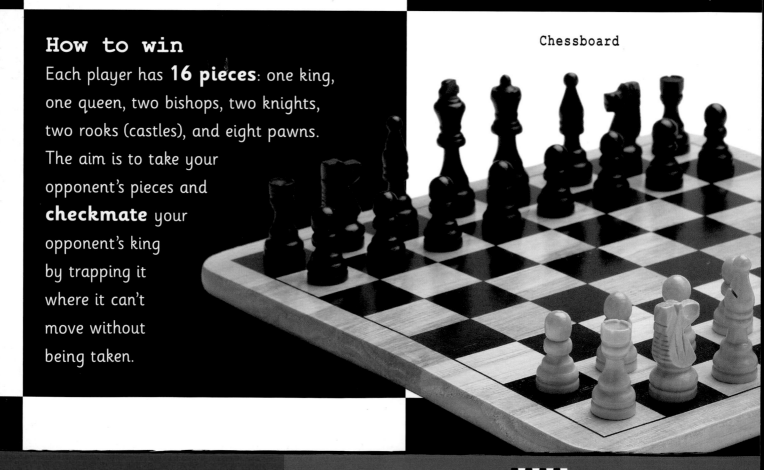

Chessboard

FACT FILE　　　Type of sport:　　　Board game

Bishop   Queen   King

Bishops can travel any distance, but must move diagonally.

World-class chess champions are called "Grandmasters".

In 1886, Wilhelm Steinitz, who was born in modern-day Czech Republic, became the first official chess world champion.

Different directions

Each piece can only move in a certain way. The **queen** is the most powerful piece because she can move any distance in any direction.

Chess history

Chess is thought to come from the **Indian** game **chaturanga**, which was first played around 1,500 years ago. The official rules used today were decided in the 1880s.

In the Middle Ages, chess was used to teach war strategy.

Number of players: 2

Equipment: Chessboard and pieces

Go

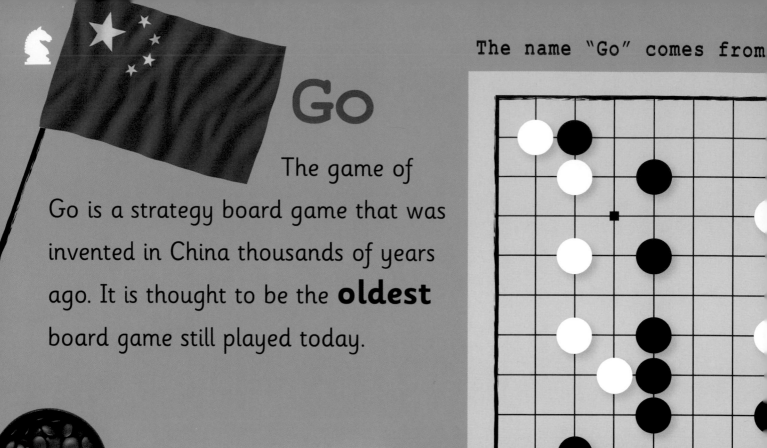

The game of Go is a strategy board game that was invented in China thousands of years ago. It is thought to be the **oldest** board game still played today.

How to play

Players take turns placing their pieces (called "stones") on a board with a grid. One player uses black stones and the other player uses white stones.

Stones can only be placed on empty points of the grid. Once a stone has been placed, it can only be removed when it has been captured by the opponent.

If a stone is surrounded on two sides, either horizontally or vertically, by the opponent's stones, it is "captured" and kept as a "prisoner".

The winner is the player that gains the most captured stones and territory of the board.

154

Gaining territory

The **territory** a player has gained at the end of the game is the number of points on the grid that are surrounded by their stones.

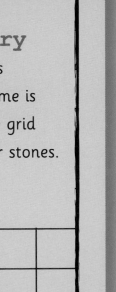

"board game of surrounding".

Tactics

Players need to pay attention to which stones can be captured. A major part of Go is the ability to **plan ahead**.

The Ko rule

One of the main rules in Go is called the **Ko rule**. This rule says players are not allowed to make a move that returns the game to its previous position. This stops the game going on too long.

In 2016 a computer program using Artificial Intelligence successfully defeated Go master Lee Sedol of Korea.

Sporting stories

All around the world, people look up to athletes because they show us that if we work hard we can do amazing things. From the peak of Mount Everest to the waves of Hawaii, here are some amazing stories about some of the most inspiring moments in **sporting history**.

The first marathon

At 42.2km (26.22 miles), the marathon is the **longest** athletics race. Its name comes from an old Greek story about a soldier called **Pheidippides**.

Battle news

According to an ancient Greek legend, in **490BCE**, Pheidippides ran all the way from the battlefield of **Marathon** to Athens, Greece, to let the city know that the Greek army had defeated their enemy. He ran the entire distance of around **40km (25 miles)**.

A marathon was held at the first modern Olympics in Athens in 1896. Greek athlete Spyridon Louis won the race in 2 hours, 58 minutes, 20 seconds.

After delivering the good news to Athens, Pheidippides is said to have died of exhaustion from his long run.

Ethiopia's Abebe Bikila is the only marathon runner to win two gold medals in a row at the Olympics.

Marathons are run all over the world, even in **ANTARCTICA**.

Keep on running!
Spanish athlete **Ricardo Abad** ran an incredible **607 marathons** in **607 days** between 1 October 2010 and 12 February 2012.

Kenya's Eliud Kipchoge broke the 2-hour marathon record with a time of 1 hour, 59 minutes, 40 seconds. Kenya's Brigid Kosgei holds the women's world record with a time of 2 hours, 14 minutes, 4 seconds.

Climbing Everest

Reaching 8,848m (29,029ft) into the sky, Mount Everest is the world's tallest mountain. For years, adventurers tried to climb it – but who was **first**?

It takes about 2 months to reach

People who climb Everest need to take oxygen tanks to help them breathe.

Oxygen → mask

Race to the top

In 1856 people worked out Everest was the world's highest mountain. From then on, the **race was on** to see who could climb it first.

Difficult ascent

Everest is in the Himalayas. It's steep, cold, and so tall there's barely any oxygen near the peak. Many climbers tried and failed to reach the top. One, George Mallory, was once asked why he would attempt such a dangerous climb. He replied. **"Because it's there"**.

We only spent 15 minutes at the peak before heading back down.

The roof of the world

On 29 May 1953, **Edmund Hillary** and **Tenzing Norgay** were the first people to reach the summit. Since then, more than 7,000 people have followed in their footsteps.

Edmund Hillary was a climber and explorer from New Zealand. He continued adventuring late into his life.

Tenzing Norgay was born near the Himalayas and was a very experienced climber. He founded a company helping others climb Everest.

Sadly, Mount Everest has become covered in litter and crowded, making it even more dangerous.

Japan's Yuichiro Miura (aged 80) is the oldest person to reach the summit.

First perfect 10

At the 1976 Olympics in Montréal, Canada, the Romanian gymnast **Nadia Comăneci** stunned the world by receiving the first **perfect score** in Olympic history.

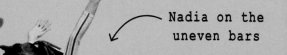

Nadia on the uneven bars

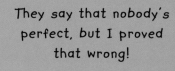

They say that nobody's perfect, but I proved that wrong!

Nobody like Nadia

Nadia was only 14 years old when she competed at the Olympics. She performed her routine on the **uneven bars** event and was incredible. When she finished, the crowd eagerly awaited her score. But something wasn't right – she had only scored 1.0...

After Nadia's performance on the uneven bars, she scored six more perfect 10s at the 1976 Olympics. She also won two gold medals at the 1980 Olympics, then retired and moved to the USA in 1989.

Achievements

5 Olympic gold medals
1976 – all-around
1976 – uneven bars
1976 – balance beam
1980 – balance beam
1980 – floor exercise

2 World Championship gold medals
1978 – balance beam
1979 – team

Score

1.00

...Getting a perfect score was thought to be impossible, so the scoreboard wasn't built to go up to 10! So instead, it read 1.00.

The crowd was confused at first, but once people realized that 1.00 meant 10.00, the arena erupted in applause!

She was amazing, why did she only score 1.00?

The four-minute mile

For years, so many athletes had tried and failed to run a mile in **less than four minutes**, that most people thought it was physically impossible and couldn't be done.

Roger Bannister

The record breaker

On May 1954, **Roger Bannister**, a medical student at Oxford University, England, finally managed to do it and proved everyone wrong.

Bannister proved that if you work hard you can achieve anything.

Achieving the impossible

On the day of the race, Bannister reached the three-quarter-mile mark in **3 minutes 0.7** seconds. This spurred him on, and, using every bit of energy he had, he managed to stagger over the finishing line in **3 minutes 59.4 seconds**.

There's no such thing as impossible!

Making history

When the results were called out, the announcer said **"3 minutes a—"**. Before the sentence ended, the crowd went wild. **History had been made!**

- The four-minute mile has since been broken by more than 1,400 athletes.

- In 1999, Morocco's Hicham El Guerrouj set the world record for the mile, completing it in 3 minutes 43.13 seconds.

Jesse Owens at the Olympics

In a time where racism was widespread, Jesse Owens proved **Olympic heroes** come from all walks of life, regardless of the colour of their skin.

Olympic Stadium

In **1936**, the **Olympic Games** were held in Germany's capital, **Berlin**. Around the same time, Adolf Hitler and the Nazi party rose to power, so tensions were high.

The 1936 Olympics were the first to be shown **live on tv**. The Nazis wanted to use the event to spread their racist belief that white people were better than everyone else.

But America's **Jesse Owens** proved them wrong in a big way. He won **three individual gold medals** in the 100m, 200m, and long jump, and a **fourth** as part of the US men's relay team.

Jesse's heroic performance sent an inspirational message to the rest of the world.

Although it angered the Nazis, most of the **German crowd** found Owens' performance **amazing** and **cheered him on**.

Owens' feat of winning four athletics gold medals didn't happen again until USA's Carl Lewis did it in 1984.

The land speed record

Ever since cars were invented, they've become faster and faster. This means people are constantly competing to see who can drive the **fastest**.

When Andy Green set the record, he went so fast he travelled faster than the speed of sound. This created an explosion called "a sonic boom".

The challenge

People were racing long before the idea of a speed record came about, but the official speed record rules state that a car has to be driven on a **flat course** over 1km (now 1 mile) in both directions. The time recorded would be the average top speed of **both times**.

Setting the pace

In 1898, Frenchman Gaston de Chasseloup-Laubat, drove an **electric car**, and reached **62.78kph (39.24mph)**. Ever since, people have continued to try and set a new record.

In 1904, France's Louis Rigolly became the first person to drive at more than 100mph.

X-43A

The air speed record is a massive 11,764.3kph (7,310mph) set by the X-43A jet – a plane without a pilot.

The water speed record is held by Australia's Ken Warby. He reached a speed of 511.09kph (317.58mph).

Thrust SSC

The fastest speed on two wheels is 605.698KPH (376.363MPH) by American ROCKY ROBINSON.

In 1927, Britain's Henry Segrave became the first to drive at more than 200mph.

The current record is 1,227.986kph (763.035mph). It was set in 1997 by Britain's Andy Green in a jet-powered car called Thrust SSC.

Eddie Aikau

Eddie Aikau was a surfer and lifeguard from Hawaii, USA who is remembered as a **Hawaiian hero** and **surfing legend**.

As a **lifeguard**, Eddie used his surfboard to help people in trouble. He rescued more than 500 people and not a single person drowned on his beach despite the dangerous waves. Eddie became famous for his brave rescues.

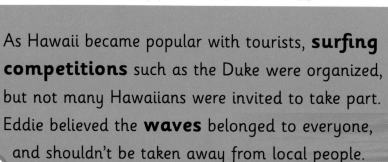

As Hawaii became popular with tourists, **surfing competitions** such as the Duke were organized, but not many Hawaiians were invited to take part. Eddie believed the **waves** belonged to everyone, and shouldn't be taken away from local people.

During the Duke competition, he surfed in behind the contestants and impressed everyone so much he was invited to take part next time. His brother Clyde won in 1973, and Eddie **won** in 1977.

Eddie surfed waves that were 12m (40ft) high!

A big-wave competition called "the Eddie" is staged each year in his honour.

Lost at sea

In 1978, Eddie and a crew set off in a canoe on a voyage to Tahiti. The canoe was caught in a storm and started to leak. Eddie paddled out on his board to **find help**.

A few hours later, the canoe was spotted by a plane and the crew was **rescued**. But sadly, Eddie was never seen again.

Eddie's memory lives on today. All across Hawaii, the phrase "Eddie Would Go" is used to describe being willing to take a risk and do the right thing.

Swimming across the Channel

The Channel is a 36km (21-mile) wide **stretch of sea** between Britain and France. In 1875, **Matthew Webb** became the first person to swim across it successfully.

Dover

Great Britain

English Channel

France

On the 24 August 1875, Englishman Matthew Webb dived into the sea in Dover, England.

More people have reached the top of Mount Everest than have swum the Channel.

In 1926, American **Gertrude Ederle** became the first woman to complete the swim.

Webb headed for France, followed by three small escort boats.

AUGUST
24
1875

On his way he battled strong currents and jellyfish stings, but kept on swimming.

21 hours 45 minutes later, he arrived exhausted but triumphant in France.

Cap
Gris-Nez

Made to swim

Swimming across the Channel was thought to be impossible, but Matthew was no ordinary swimmer. He learned to swim from an early age and spent many years as a **sailor**.

In 2012, Australia's **Trent Grimsey** completed the swim in **6 hours and 55 minutes**.

Britain's **Alison Streeter** has completed the swim an astonishing **46 times**.

Amazing **athletes**

There are good athletes, and then there are the **best of the best**. From breaking records to winning gold medals, these athletes are just built to win. Let's take a look at some of the top athletes of all time in this sporting hall of fame.

Serena Williams

Born in 1981, America's Serena Williams is one of the most **successful** tennis players to ever grace the court.

A talent for tennis

Serena started playing tennis at the age of **three**. She turned professional at **14** and, four years later, won her first **Grand Slam**. It would not be her last!

A is for ace,
B is for ball,
C is for champion!

The greatest

This was the start of a **stunning career**. By 2019, she had won **23** Grand Slam singles titles, **14** Grand Slam doubles titles, and been the world's top-ranked female player for **319** weeks of her career.

Serena has also won four Olympic gold medals.

Serena's sister Venus is also one of the best players ever. When they teamed up in doubles they were almost unstoppable.

Career highlights

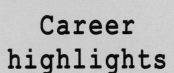

She has won the US Open six times, the Australian Open seven times, the French Open three times, and Wimbledon seven times.

She was ranked world number 1 for 186 weeks in a row.

1

33

She has reached 33 Grand Slam singles finals, and won 23 of them.

She played against her sister Venus in nine Grand Slam singles finals. She won seven of them.

9

She is the highest-earning female athlete of all time.

On top of being a tennis legend, she is a successful fashion designer.

Tiger Woods

Born in the USA in 1975, Eldrick **"Tiger"** Woods is one of the most famous and successful athletes ever. Not just in golf, but in any sport.

Little tiger

Coached by this father, Tiger started playing golf at the **age of two** and showed huge talent right away. He was so good, he was invited to be on television to show off his golf skills the same year.

The master of Masters

After competing in junior tournaments and turning professional, Tiger became a global superstar in 1997 by winning the **Masters**, one of golf's biggest tournaments, by a record-breaking 12 shots, when he only 21.

Career highlights

15 He has won 15 major golf titles.

He is one of only five players to have won all four of golf's major championships. **5**

81 He has won 81 PGA (Professional Golfer's Association) Tour titles.

He was ranked the world's number 1 player for 281 weeks in a row between 2008 and 2010.

20 He has scored 20 hole-in-ones throughout his career.

His success has earned him more than $1 billion!

5 He has won the Masters five times.

Shaun White

Born in California in 1986, Shaun White took up snowboarding when he was **six** years old. He went on to become the most **successful** snowboarder in history.

His nickname is "The Flying Tomato" because when he burst on the scene he had very long red hair.

Triple gold

Shaun won **gold medals** at the 2006 and 2010 Winter Olympics. In 2018, he won gold again, becoming the first snowboarder ever to win **three** gold medals.

White performed so well on his first two runs in 2010 he knew he would win even if he failed his McTwist – but he still wanted to show it to the crowd!

Tricky!

One of the highlights of Shaun's career was pulling off a very difficult trick called the **"Double McTwist 1260"** at the 2010 Winter Olympics. The trick involves **two flips** and **three and a half spins** at once!

Career highlights

7
TODAY

He won his first snowboard competition at the age of seven.

He became a national champion for the first time in 2003, when he was just 16 years old! **16**

3 He is the first snowboarder in history to win three Olympic golds.

13

He holds the record for snowboarding gold medals at the X Games tournament, with 13.

He is also a professional skateboarder.

Lindsey Vonn

American Lindsey Vonn is one of the most exciting and **successful** skiers in history. She has more victories than any other female skier.

After winning her eighth World Championships medal, Lindsey retired in 2019.

Family business

Lindsey's father and grandfather were both competitive skiers. She followed in their ski tracks and took to the slopes when she was just **two** years old! By nine she was competing internationally.

Iron will

Lindsey's success has never come easily. She had to overcome several serious **injuries** that almost ended her career, but she worked hard and came back to win.

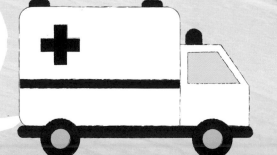

Career highlights

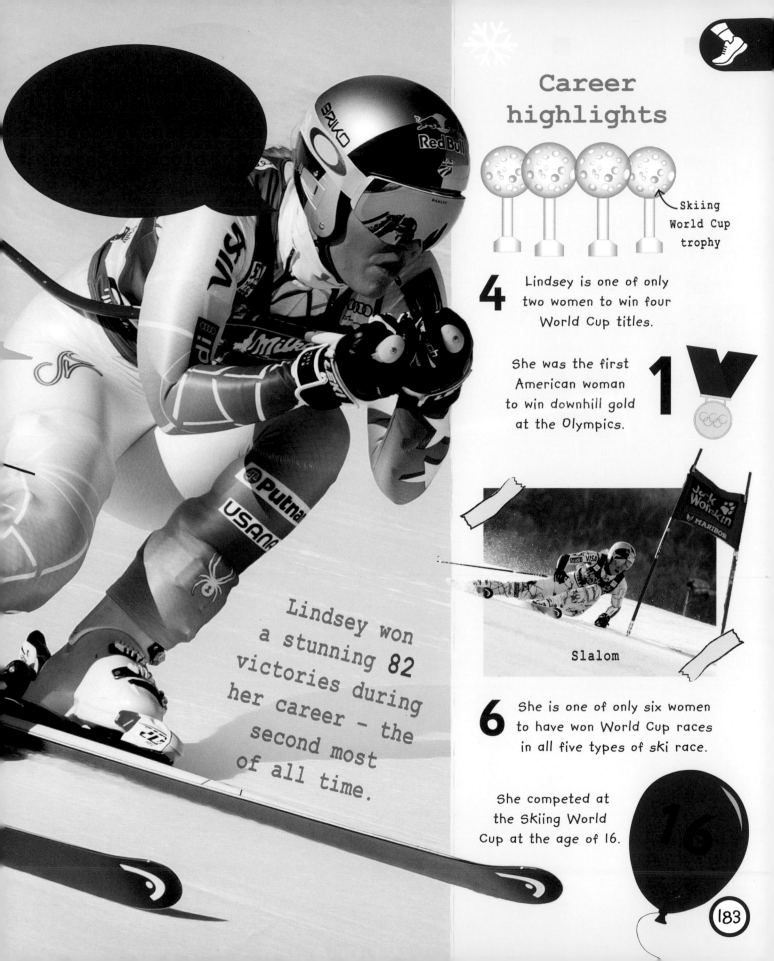

Skiing World Cup trophy

4 Lindsey is one of only two women to win four World Cup titles.

She was the first American woman to win downhill gold at the Olympics. **1**

Slalom

Lindsey won a stunning 82 victories during her career – the second most of all time.

6 She is one of only six women to have won World Cup races in all five types of ski race.

She competed at the Skiing World Cup at the age of 16. **16**

Yuna Kim

The South Korean superstar Yuna Kim is one of the best and most **loved** athletes in the world.

Yuna uses her fame and success to help others, and has donated lots of money to charity.

Pure talent

When Yuna started skating at the age of six, she had to train in old rinks and wore ill-fitting skates. But her talent shone through and she became Korea's national champion at 12 and **world junior champion** at 18.

Skating superstar

Yuna became the first woman to win **all four** of ice-skating's grand slam titles: the Winter Olympics, the World Championships, the Four Continents Championships, and the Grand Prix final.

When she was 16, Yuna moved to **VANCOUVER, CANADA**, to train on the ice rinks there.

Yuna retired after the 2014 Winter Olympics when she was just 23. Four years later, she was chosen to light the cauldron during the opening ceremony for the Winter Olympics in Korea.

At the 2010 Olympic Games in Vancouver, Yuna won gold and set a NEW WORLD RECORD.

Usain Bolt

He's not quite as fast as a bolt of lightning, but Usain Bolt is still the **fastest man** in history and the greatest sprinter of all time.

Born to run

Usain was born in Jamaica in 1986 and was a gifted sprinter from a young age. When he was 15 he won gold in the 200m at the World Junior Championships. He was the youngest world junior gold medallist ever, and he was just **getting started**...

The Lightning Bolt

Usain made history at the 2008 Olympics in Beijing, China, when he broke the 100m and 200m **world records**. He was also in record-breaking form at the 2009 World Championships in Berlin, Germany, breaking both records once again!

As a child, Usain was also a fantastic cricket and football player.

Usain took his famous celebration pose from a Jamaican tourist advert. It means "to the world".

Usain donated money to protect animals in Kenya, such as the Cheetah – the fastest land animal on Earth.

Usain once set the 100m world record even though one of his shoelaces was untied.

Career highlights

9.58 He holds the 100m world record of 9.58 seconds.

He holds the 200m world record of 19.19 seconds. **19.19**

8 He has 8 Olympic gold medals.

11 He won 11 gold medals at the World Championships.

His career top speed is 27.8mph (44.72kph). **27.8**

He's still not as fast as me!

He's the fastest person in human history!

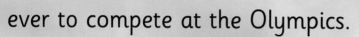

Won at Athens in 2004

Won at Beijing in 2008

Michael Phelps

With **23 gold medals**, American swimmer Michael Phelps is the most successful athlete ever to compete at the Olympics.

During training, Michael swam for around five hours every day.

The rise of Phelps

Michael started swimming at the age of seven, and qualified for the 2000 Olympic Games when he was just **15 years old**. His record-breaking streak began four years later.

Going for gold

Michael won **six gold medals** at the 2004 Olympics. Four years later, he set the record for most gold medals won at a single games with **eight**. The gold rush continued with **four** in 2012, and the superstar ended his career in style by winning **five** in 2016.

Fuel for the machine

All that swimming takes a lot of energy. Michael's eating habits are the stuff of legend. This is what he ate every day while training for the 2008 Olympics.

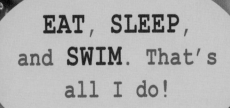

EAT, SLEEP, and SWIM. That's all I do!

A five-egg omelet

Two cups of coffee

Three fried egg, ham, and cheese sandwiches

A pizza

Two ham and cheese sandwiches

Three chocolate-chip pancakes

A bowl of grits

Energy drinks

Slices of French toast

Two bowls of pasta

Muhammad **Ali**

Also known as **"The Greatest"**, Muhammad Ali was one of the most famous boxers of all time and one of the **best-known figures** of the 20th century.

Ali used to predict which round he would win his fights in, and was often right!

Cassius Clay

Muhammad was born as **Cassius Clay** and took up boxing at age 12. He became famous when he won a **gold medal** at the 1960 Olympics.

Name change

After returning from the Olympics, he changed his name to **Muhammad Ali** and became world heavyweight champion for the first time in **1964**, winning the Championship belt.

World Championship belt

Around 1 BILLION people watched his famous "Rumble in the Jungle" fight.

Ali's boxing style was all about speed. He famously said he "floats like a butterfly and stings like a bee".

Boxing legend

He was stripped of his titles in 1967 after **refusing to fight** in the Vietnam War because of his religion. But he returned to boxing in 1970 and went on to win **two** more titles.

Muhammad Ali is a hero to many, not just for his boxing skills, but for standing up for what he believed in.

Lin Dan

China's Lin Dan started playing badminton when he was just five years old. He grew up to become the greatest player of **all time** and a sporting icon.

World Championships

Olympic Games

has won the

Lin Dan

Lin was born in Longyan, China, in 1983.

The greatest

Lin became a professional badminton player as a teenager, and by the time he was 19 he was **world number one**. He holds many records, including being the only men's player to win back to back Olympic titles.

192

All England Open

World Cup

Thomas Cup

Asian Championships

Asian Games

Sudirman Cup

Super Series Masters Finals

Lin's parents wanted him to play the piano when he was young, but he gave that up to focus on badminton.

World Championships FIVE TIMES!

Super Dan's Super Slam
Famously nicknamed **"Super Dan"** by one of his rivals, Lin is the only player in history to win **all nine** of badminton's major titles (known as the Super Slam).

Lionel Messi

Lionel Messi is thought of by many as the finest football player of his generation and, by some, as the **best of all time**.

Early life

Lionel was born in **Argentina** in 1987. As a child he suffered from a medical problem that slowed his growth. However, it was clear Lionel was super talented, and at 12, he was given a try-out by the Spanish club Barcelona.

Barcelona was so impressed by Lionel's skill that they offered to pay for his medicine.

Messi's nickname is "The Flea" because his quick, darting style makes him a pest to defenders!

Lionel Messi has played more than 600 games

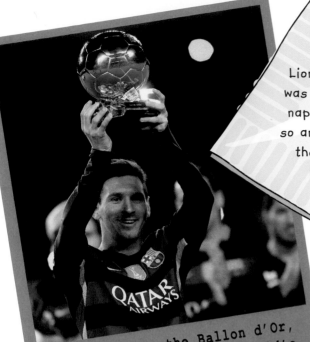

Messi has won the Ballon d'Or, the award given to the world's best player, five times.

Lionel's first contract was written on a paper napkin! Barcelona was so amazed at his talent, they wanted to sign him right away.

Lionel moved to Spain and signed with Barcelona. The rest is history!

Career of a champion

Lionel made his debut for Barcelona aged 17 and has gone on to win a staggering number of titles with the club, including the Spanish league title ten times and the Champions League four times.

in his career with **Barcelona.**

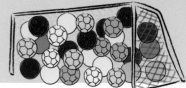

91 In 2012, he scored 91 goals for Barcelona and Argentina.

9 He has won the award for the best player in the Spanish league a record nine times.

400 He is the only player to score more than 400 goals in the Spanish league.

68 He is Argentina's all-time top goalscorer, with 68.

21 In 2012 and 2013, he scored in 21 Spanish league matches in a row.

10 Like many football legends, he wears the number 10.

Donald
Bradman

Australian Donald Bradman is a cricketing **legend**. One of his records is so impressive, it's called one of the greatest achievements in any sport.

Batting average

99.94

Batting average

In cricket and baseball, batting average measures how **successful** a batsman is. In cricket, it's the number of runs scored divided by the number of times the batsmen is gotten out.

The next best average after Donald's 99.94 is 61.87, by Australia's Adam Voges.

The Don

Donald first played for Australia in 1928, aged 20, and became the best batsman in the game. He was almost unstoppable during his 20 year career.

Donald became a national icon in Australia. He even had a stamp and coin made in his honour.

Australia

Sir Donald Bradman
20 cents

← Adam Voges

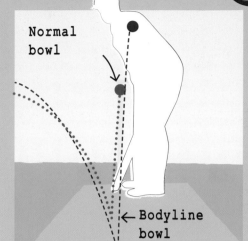

Normal bowl

← Bodyline bowl

Beating bodyline

To try to beat Donald, Australia's rival, England, resorted to a tactic called "bodyline" (aiming at the batsman instead of the wicket). They won that game, but Donald had the last laugh. He never lost to England again.

LeBron James

Known as **"King James"**, LeBron James is considered to be one of the best **basketball** players of all time.

LeBron was born in Ohio, USA. It was clear from a young age he was very talented. By age 16 he was on the cover of magazines around the country.

The rise of the king

When he was 18, LeBron became the **youngest player** to be chosen first in the NBA (National Basketball Association) draft. Best of all, he was picked by his local team the **Cleveland Cavaliers**, and quickly became one of the game's best players.

Team change

After several years playing in Cleveland, he moved to the **Miami Heat** and won two NBA Championships in 2012 and 2013. He rejoined the **Cavaliers** in 2014 and led them to their first-ever Championship in 2016, before joining the **LA Lakers** in 2018.

LeBron is also famous for helping others. He has set up a school called "I Promise" in his hometown of Akron, Ohio, to help children in need.

Career highlights

1
Youngest player to be the number 1 pick in the NBA draft.

2
Two Olympic gold medals with USA's basketball team.

3
Three-time NBA Champion.

4
Currently fourth on the NBA's all-time points-scoring list.

4
Voted the NBA's Most Valuable Player four times.

199

Sporting events

What do you get when you bring the best teams and players **together**? Lots and lots of exciting competitions! All over the world, people come together to take part or watch athletes compete in special events. The aim is to see who is the best, but mostly, it's a lot of fun!

The Olympics

The Summer Olympic Games is the world's most famous **sporting event**. The top athletes from around the world come together to see who is the best of the **best**.

More than just sport

Although the sport is the main reason to come together, the Olympics is special for more than just the competition. It's a time when the whole world **celebrates** together.

Old and new

The Olympics were inspired by ancient Olympic Games held in Greece many years ago. Frenchman **Pierre de Coubertin** was the driving force behind bringing the Olympics back.

The modern games were held for the first time in Athens, Greece, in 1896.

Pierre de Coubertin

The Olympics in figures:

Held every **4** years

33 different sports

339 events

1 huge celebration!

The 2020 games in Tokyo was the first

1988
Seoul,
Korea

1992
Barcelona,
Spain

1996
Atlanta,
USA

2000
Sydney,
Australia

2004
Athens,
Greece

2008
Beijing,
China

2012
London,
UK

2016
Rio de
Janeiro,
Brazil

2020
Tokyo,
Japan

Hosting

The Olympics are held every four years, and are staged in a different **city** each time to symbolize countries working together and to celebrate different cultures.

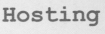

Olympic flame

A **torch** carrying fire from the site of the ancient games in Olympia, Greece, is passed from person to person, all the way to where the games are held. The torch is used to light a big fire that burns during the Olympic games.

At the first modern Olympics, winners were awarded an olive branch. But since 1904 they are given gold, silver, and bronze medals for coming first, second, and third.

American swimmer Michael Phelps is the most successful Olympic athlete in history. He won an amazing 23 gold medals during his career.

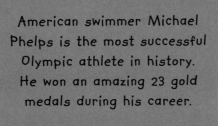

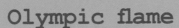
games to have **SKATEBOARDING** as an Olympic sport.

The Winter Olympics

Just like the Summer Games, the Winter Olympic Games are held every **four years**. But all the sports take place on **snow** and **ice**.

The Winter Games have been held in 12 different countries across Europe, North America, and Asia.

History of the Games
The Games were held for the first time in 1924, in **Chamonix**, France. Until 1992, the Summer and Winter Games were held in the **same year**, but now run two years apart.

Ice hockey

Past
The 2018 Winter Olympic Games where held in **Pyeongchang, South Korea**, and included:

from **92** countries

across **7** sports

2,833 competitors

competing in **102** events

50 of which involved skiing

| 1994 Lillehammer, Norway | 1998 Nagano, Japan | 2002 Salt Lake City, USA | 2006 Turin, Italy | 2010 Vancouver, Canada | 2014 Sochi, Russia | 2018 Pyeongchang, South Korea | 2022 Beijing, China |

Bobsleigh

Marit Bjørgen

Norwegian dominance

No country has performed as well at the Winter Olympics as **Norway**. Norwegian athletes lead the all-time medal table, in both gold medals (132) and overall medals (368).

Norwegian cross-country skier Marit Bjørgen is the most successful Winter Olympian ever. She has won 15 medals (8 golds).

Future

The 2022 games will be held in **Beijing, China**. 109 events will take place across seven sports:

Biathlon
Bobsleigh
Curling
Ice hockey

Luge
Skating
Skiing

The Paralympic Games

The Paralympics are an **international sports competition** for disabled athletes held every four years. There are both Summer and Winter Paralympics.

Origins

In 1948, Sir Ludwig Guttmann organized a sports competition at a hospital in England for soldiers who had suffered disabilities while fighting during **World War II**. Four years later, competitors from the Netherlands joined the Games and the Paralympic movement was born.

Most of the sports played at the Paralympics are the same as the ones at the Olympics. But a few, such as "goalball" and "boccia", are unique to the Paralympics.

American Trischa Zorn is the most successful Paralympian in history. She won an amazing 41 gold medals in swimming between 1980 and 2004.

The games

The first games for disabled athletes were held in Rome, Italy, in 1960. Today, the Paralympics are staged at the **same place** as the Summer and Winter Olympic Games, and are an important part of the world's sporting calendar.

The "Para" in "Paralympics" comes from the Greek word "para", which means "next to", because the Paralympics run alongside the Olympics.

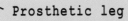

Prosthetic leg

The events

The Paralympics feature more than 20 sports and hundreds of events, including athletics, wheelchair basketball, cycling, swimming, and wheelchair fencing. The athletes range from those who are blind, to those who have lost a limb or are confined to a wheelchair, and many more.

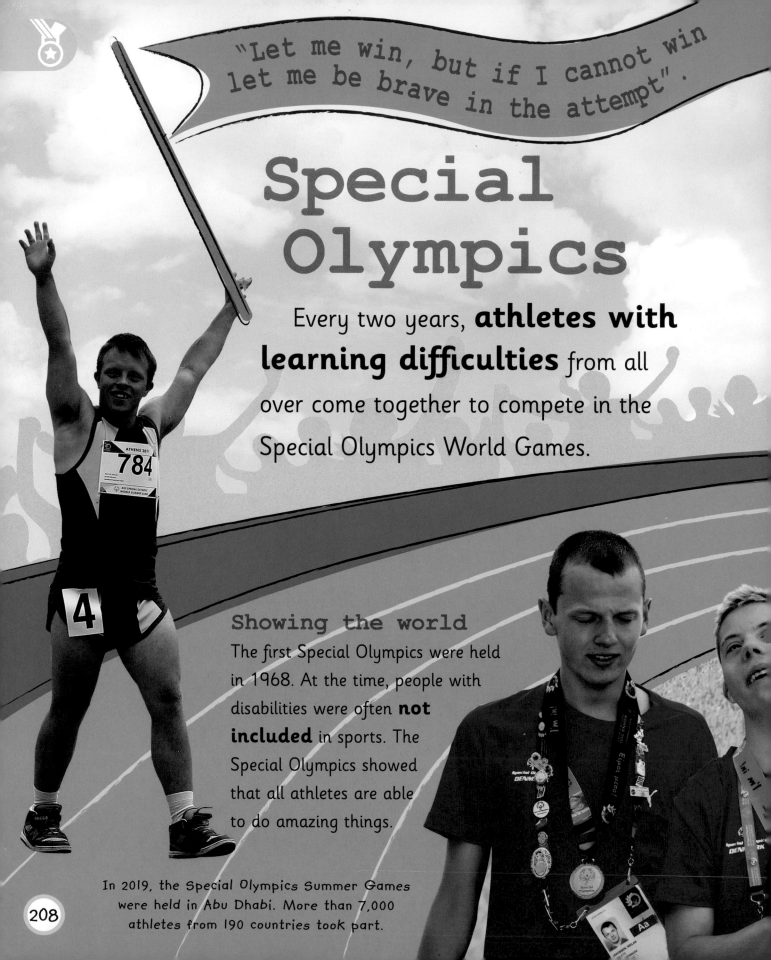

"Let me win, but if I cannot win let me be brave in the attempt".

Special Olympics

Every two years, **athletes with learning difficulties** from all over come together to compete in the Special Olympics World Games.

Showing the world

The first Special Olympics were held in 1968. At the time, people with disabilities were often **not included** in sports. The Special Olympics showed that all athletes are able to do amazing things.

In 2019, the Special Olympics Summer Games were held in Abu Dhabi. More than 7,000 athletes from 190 countries took part.

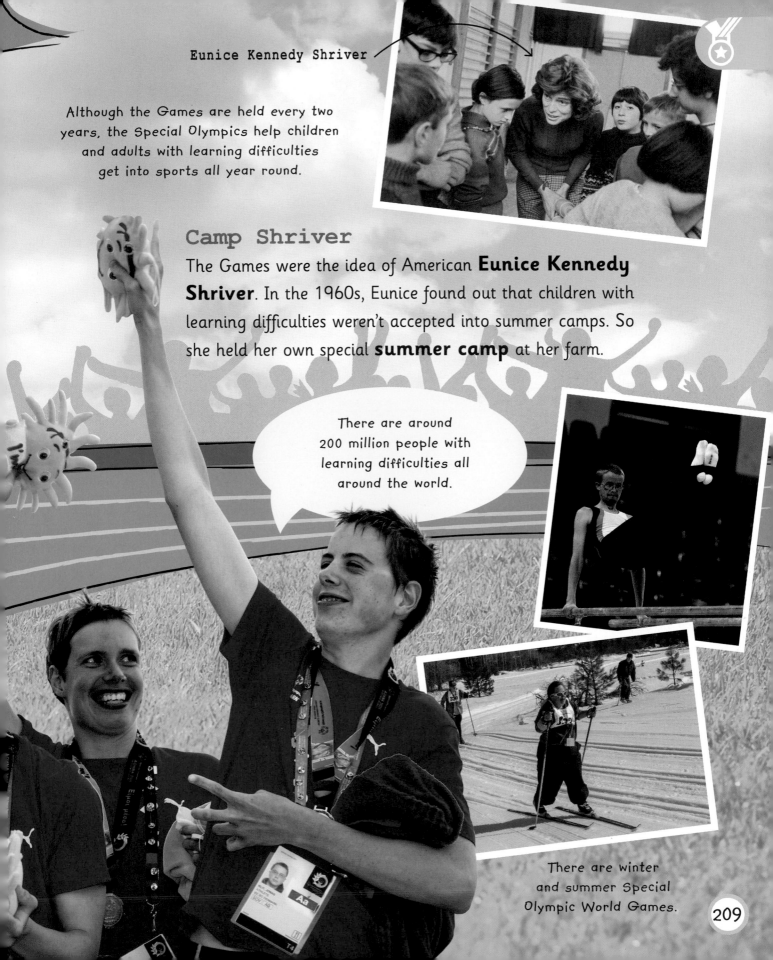

Eunice Kennedy Shriver

Although the Games are held every two years, the Special Olympics help children and adults with learning difficulties get into sports all year round.

Camp Shriver

The Games were the idea of American **Eunice Kennedy Shriver**. In the 1960s, Eunice found out that children with learning difficulties weren't accepted into summer camps. So she held her own special **summer camp** at her farm.

There are around 200 million people with learning difficulties all around the world.

There are winter and summer Special Olympic World Games.

209

The World Cup

The World Cup is a huge **international football** tournament held every **four years** to decide which country's team is the best.

The world's biggest stage

There's nothing that captures people's attention more than the World Cup. Around **3.5 billion** people watched the 2018 World Cup. That's around **half of all the people in the world!**

Stages

The World Cup was first held in **1930** in Uruguay. The competition is made up of two parts: a **group stage** and a **knockout phase**. 32 teams play for a chance to win, but from 2026, 48 teams will enter.

The World Cup trophy

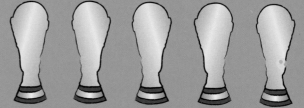

Brazil have won the World Cup a record five times.

Only eight countries have
won the men's World Cup:

Brazil
(five times)

Italy
(four times)

Germany
(four times)

France
(two times)

Uruguay
(two times)

Argentina
(two times)

England
(one time)

Spain
(one time)

Only four countries have won
the Women's World Cup:

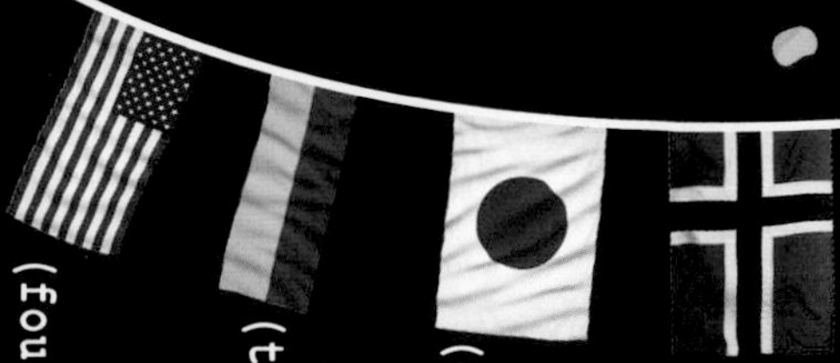

USA
(four times)

Germany
(two times)

Japan
(one time)

Norway
(one time)

Women's World Cup

The FIFA Women's World Cup was first held in **1991**.
Like the men's competition, it is staged every four years.
The **United States** have been the most successful
team, winning **four times**.

The Super Bowl

The Super Bowl is the game that decides the **American football** champion. 32 teams compete for it, but only one can win.

All or nothing

The Super Bowl is played on the first Sunday of February after a 16-game season followed by **playoff** games where teams are knocked out when they lose. The last two remaining teams face off in the Super Bowl.

The 2015 Super Bowl between the New England Patriots and Seattle Seahawks was watched by 114.4 million people!

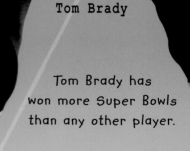

Tom Brady

Tom Brady has won more Super Bowls than any other player.

The prize

The trophy given to the Super Bowl winner is the "Vince Lombardi Trophy". It's named after the legendary **coach** who won the first two Super Bowls.

Vince Lombardi Trophy

During halftime, musicians perform a spectacular concert and companies pay millions to advertise during breaks.

Green Bay Packers

Kansas City Chiefs

Sunday showdown

The first Super Bowl was played in 1961 between the **Green Bay Packers** and **Kansas City Chiefs**. The day of the Super Bowl has become known as **"Super Bowl Sunday"**.

Indianapolis 500

The Indianapolis 500, also known as the **Indy 500**, is the world's **oldest motor race**. It was first held in 1911.

History of the Indy

The race is held every May at the Indianapolis Motor Speedway in Indiana, USA. The race is long and tiring, and takes around **three hours** to finish. Drivers need to be skilled and have great concentration.

Vroom! Vroom!

Why 500?

The oval-shaped circuit is **4km (2.5 miles)** long. Drivers race **200 laps**, which is a distance of **805km (500 miles)**. That's why it's called the Indy 500!

The race was shown on **TELEVISION** for the first time in **1965**. Before that, it could only be followed on the **RADIO**.

Every year since the 1930s, the winner of the race celebrates by drinking a bottle of milk or pouring it over their head!

The Indy 500, the Monaco Grand Prix, and 24 Hours of Le Mans make up "The Triple Crown of Motorsport".

Most wins

Three American drivers are tied for the record of most wins, with **four.**

A.J. Foyt

Al Unser

Rick Mears

Tour de France

The Tour de France is the most famous cycling event in the world. It's **very difficult** and **tiring**, with some parts taking place on mountains.

On your bike

The race is made up of different **stages**. Overall, it takes three weeks and goes for thousands of miles. The route is different every year, but it always finishes in Paris.

While most of the race takes place in France, sometimes

Eddy Merckx from Belgium, Bernard Hinault and Jacques Anquetil from France, and Miguel Induráin from Spain, have all won the Tour de France **five times**.

Eddy Merckx →

Eddy Merckx is a cycling legend. He holds the record for **most stage wins** in the Tour de France, with 34.

Jerseys

Riders who are leading certain categories wear special **coloured jerseys** during the race:

The race's leading sprinter wears green.

The overall leader wears yellow.

The leading rider in the mountain stages wears polka dots.

The first Tour de France was in 1903. Cyclists stopped at cafes to rest.

the stages pass through other countries.

In 1989, after 3,285km (2,041 miles), the winner, Greg LeMond, finished just **8 seconds** ahead of the cyclist behind him. It was the **closest race** in Tour de France history.

Frenchman Sylvain Chavanel holds the record for Tour de France **appearances**, with 18.

Sylvain Chavanel

The Grand Slams

The tennis season is built around **four** major tournaments known as "Grand Slams". To win each Slam, players must win seven straight matches against the best players in the world.

The Australian Open

Played in Melbourne in January, the Australian Open used to be played on grass, but is now played on a **hard court**.

Germany's Steffi Graf set a record by reaching 13 Grand Slam finals in a row.

Steffi Graf

The French Open

The **red clay** surface of the French Open slows the ball and makes it **bounce higher**. This is good for players who strike the ball with lots of power. It's played in Paris in June.

Rafael Nadal

Spain's Rafael Nadal is the king of clay. He has won the French Open an extraordinary 12 times!

Around 50,000 balls are used at each of the Grand Slams!

The most successful men's and women's singles players are Switzerland's Roger Federer, with 20 titles, and Australia's Margaret Court, with 24.

Wimbledon

The oldest and most famous Grand Slam is Wimbledon, played in July in England. It's the only slam played on **grass**, which is the **fastest** and least bouncy tennis surface.

Fred Perry

Only eight men and ten women have won all four Grand Slams. The first to achieve this was Britain's Fred Perry.

The US Open

Naomi Osaka

Like the Australian Open, the US Open is played on a **hard court**, which is faster than clay but slower than grass. It's played in New York in September.

Index

Acknowledgements

The publisher would like to thank the following for their kind permission to reproduce their photographs:

Key: a= above; b=below/bottom; c=centre; f=far; l=left, r=right, t=top.

1 Alamy Stock Photo: Yolanda Oltra (cra). **Dreamstime. com:** Neil Lockhart (cb); Raja Rc / Rcmathiraj (b). **Getty Images:** Chris Elise / NBAE (l). **2 Alamy Stock Photo:** TGSPHOTO (bl). **Dreamstime.com:** Volodymyr Melnyk (br); Stephen Noakes (bc). **Getty Images:** Stanislav Krasilnikov\ TASS (cr). **2-3 Dreamstime.com:** Raja Rc / Rcmathiraj (b). **3 123RF.com:** Roman Stetsyk (cb). **Alamy Stock Photo:** Artokoloro Quint Lox Limited (cl). **Dreamstime.com:** Skypixel (cr). **iStockphoto.com:** pidjoe (bl). **4 Dreamstime. com:** Sergeyoch (tr); Roman Stetsyk (cb). **Getty Images:** Baptiste Fernandez / Icon Sport (br). **5 Dreamstime.com:** Artisticco Llc (tr). **Getty Images:** TF-Images (bc). **6 123RF. com:** Fabio Pagani (cb). **Alamy Stock Photo:** Cultura Creative (RF) (br); sportpoint (clb). **Dreamstime.com:** Walter Arce (bc). **Getty Images:** Wally McNamee / Corbis (cra). **7 Getty Images:** Ben Stansall / AFP (tl); Denis Doyle (crb); TPN (bc). **8 Dreamstime.com:** Branchecarica (cla); Vladimir Kulakov (c). **Getty Images:** Foto Olimpik / NurPhoto (cla/ Speedway). **8-9 123RF.com:** Marina Scurupii (Background). **9 Dreamstime.com:** Petesaloutos (ca); Skypixel (bc). **Getty Images:** Jamie McDonald (cl). **12-13 Dreamstime.com:** Montypeter (Background). **13 Alamy Stock Photo:** Entertainment Pictures (cb). **14-15 Alamy Stock Photo:** Cultura Creative (RF) (c). **15 Dreamstime.com:** Volodymyr Melnyk (cl). **16 Getty Images:** Mark Brake (c). **16-17 Alamy Stock Photo:** wanderworldimages (Background). **17 Getty Images:** Michael Dodge (cla). **18-19 Getty Images:** Mike Hewitt. **19 Getty Images:** Adrian Dennis / AFP (br). **20 iStockphoto.com:** benoitb (crb). **20-21 Dreamstime. com:** Raja Rc / Rcmathiraj (cb). **21 iStockphoto.com:** pidjoe (c); strickke (cra). **22-23 Alamy Stock Photo:** Hero Images Inc. (cb). **Dreamstime.com:** Montypeter (Background). **23 Alamy Stock Photo:** Hero Images Inc. (cla). **24 Alamy Stock Photo:** TGSPHOTO (cra). **Dreamstime.com:** Wavebreakmedia Ltd (bl). **Getty Images:** Alex Davidson (l). **24-25 Dreamstime.com:** Ritu Jethani (t/Background); Raja Rc / Rcmathiraj (b/Background). **25 123RF.com:** Ilyas Dean (br). **Dreamstime.com:** Stephen Noakes (clb). **Getty Images:** Alex Davidson (crb); Michael Steele (cr). **26 Getty Images:** Juice Images (ca). **26-27 123RF.com:** Sirapob Konjay (t). **Dreamstime.com:** Rangizzz (c/Background). **27 Alamy Stock Photo:** Historic Collection (cl). **29 Dreamstime.com:** Jerry Coli (tr); Skypixel (bc, crb). **30 Getty Images:** Steve Christo / Corbis (cr). **30-31 123RF.com:** Vereshchagin Dmitry (Background). **Alamy Stock Photo:** Ilyas Ayub. **31 Dreamstime.com:** Andreykuzmin (r). **32 Dreamstime. com:** Eugene Onischenko (r). **33 123RF.com:** Volodymyr Melnyk (c). **Alamy Stock Photo:** Martin Berry (cr). **Rex by Shutterstock:** Kiyoshi Ota / EPA-EFE (cla). **34-35 Dreamstime.com:** Pixattitude (c). **35 Alamy Stock Photo:** Simon Balson (ca). **39 Alamy Stock Photo:** Age Fotostock (clb); Dipper Historic (crb). **Dorling Kindersley:** American Museum of Natural History (bc). **Dreamstime.com:** Vladimir Galkin (cl). **40-41 Dreamstime.com:** Montypeter (t). **Getty Images:** Dimitri Iundt / Corbis / VCG (bc). **40 Getty Images:** Tony Duffy / Allsport (bc); Dimitri Iundt / Corbis / VCG (tl); Alexander Hassenstein (bl); Quinn Rooney (br). **41 Getty Images:** Kamil Krzaczynski / AFP (br/New); Remy Gros / Icon Sport (bl); Dursun Aydemir / Anadolu Agency (bc). **42-43 Dreamstime.com:** Petesaloutos (c). **iStockphoto. com:** Kerrick (t/Background). **43 Alamy Stock Photo:** Federico Caputo (bl). **Getty Images:** Robert Riger (ca). **44 Dreamstime.com:** Yoshiro Mizuta (tc). **Getty Images:** Manuel Blondeau / Icon Sport (cra). **45 Alamy Stock Photo:** UpperCut Images (ca). **Getty Images:** Dimitri Iundt / Corbis / VCG (crb). **46 Dreamstime.com:** Dariusz Kopestynski / Copestello (bc); Hkratky (cl); Mitchell Gunn (cr).

47 Alamy Stock Photo: Action Plus Sports (tr). **Dreamstime.com:** Evren Kalinbacak (cl). **48 Alamy Stock Photo:** Wang Lili / Xinhua (r). **49 Alamy Stock Photo:** INTERFOTO (l); Jordi Salas (tr). **50-51 123RF.com:** Vassiliy Prikhodko (t). **Getty Images:** Cameron Spencer (c). **51 Alamy Stock Photo:** Richard Grange (cl). **Getty Images:** Lennart Preiss (crb). **52 Dreamstime.com:** Chelsdo (cra); Ukrphoto (cl); Roman Stetsyk (c); Petrjoura (crb). **53 123RF. com:** Roman Stetsyk (tl). **Dreamstime.com:** Igor Dolgov (cb); Ukrphoto (clb); Matthias Hangst / Bongarts (cb); Visual China Group (tr). **54 123RF.com:** ostill (fcra). **Dreamstime.com:** Jamie Cross / Jamie_cross (cb); Pixattitude (cra). **55 Alamy Stock Photo:** Cyclist People By Vision (ca). **Dreamstime.com:** Pixattitude (cra, tr); Rudy Umans / Rudyumans (bc). **56 Getty Images:** Dan Mullan (clb). **56-57 iStockphoto.com:** Henrik5000. **57 Getty Images:** Martin Barraud (cr); Alexander Hassenstein / Bongarts (cra). **58 123RF.com:** Abdul Razak Latif (cl); Fabio Pagani (cb). **Dreamstime.com:** Branchecarica (tr); Neil Lockhart (cb); Anan Punyod (cb/Road). **Getty Images:** MediaNews Group (bl); Ian Walton (crb). **58-59 Getty Images:** Foto Olimpik / NurPhoto (t). **59 123RF.com:** mreco99 (cr). **Dreamstime.com:** Walter Arce (br); Ievgen Soloviov (c); Pavel Boruta (cb); Anan Punyod (br/Road). **60 Getty Images:** Andy Lyons (cra). **60-61 Getty Images:** Natasha Morello / Racing Photos. **62-63 123RF.com:** Sirapob Konjay (t). **Dreamstime.com:** Andreevaee (c). **62 123RF.com:** martinkay78 (cb); Natthawut panyosaeng (cl). **63 123RF.com:** Natthawut panyosaeng (cl). **Dorling Kindersley:** Barnabas Kindersley (cla). **Getty Images:** TF-Images (cr). **64 Alamy Stock Photo:** PhotoStock-Israel (cl). **Dreamstime.com:** Eugene Onischenko (crb); Piyathep (tr). **Getty Images:** Nao Imai / Aflo (c). **65 123RF.com:** olegdudko (cb). **Alamy Stock Photo:** Ivan Okyere-Boakye Photography (tl). **Dreamstime.com:** Volodymyr Melnyk (cl). **Getty Images:** The Asahi Shimbun (c). **iStockphoto.com:** Mrbig_Photography (bc). **66 123RF.com:** Andrii Kaderov (clb). **66-67 123RF.com:** ocusfocus (c). **67 123RF.com:** Vasilis Ververidis (c). Dreamstime.com: Lumppini (tc). **68-69 Alamy Stock Photo:** Peter Llewellyn. **70 Getty Images:** Hoang Dinh Nam / AFP (r). **71 Dreamstime.com:** Kanjanee Chaisin (cla). **Getty Images:** Visual China Group. **72 123RF.com:** Attila Mittl / atee83 (cl). **72-73 Getty Images:** Baptiste Fernandez / Icon Sport. **74 Dreamstime.com:** Galina Barskaya (crb); .shock (cl). **74-75 Dreamstime.com:** Sergeyoch (c). **75 Alamy Stock Photo:** Cal Sport Media (l). **76 123RF.com:** Anan Kaewkhammul (r). **77 Dorling Kindersley:** South of England Rare Breeds Centre, Ashford, Kent (cl). **Dreamstime.com:** Pariyawit Sukumpantanasarn (cra); Zagorskid (tl, bc). **79 Alamy Stock Photo:** Cultura Creative (RF). **Getty Images:** Mike Brett / Popperfoto (cra). **80 Dorling Kindersley:** Stephen Oliver (r). **Rex by Shutterstock:** Andy Wong / AP (clb). **80-81 Dreamstime. com:** Eugene Onischenko. **81 Dorling Kindersley:** Stephen Oliver (cr). **82-83 Alamy Stock Photo:** Hemis. **83 Rex by Shutterstock:** Andrew Cowie (cl). **84 Getty Images:** Jordan Mansfield (crb). **86 123RF.com:** ammit (bc). **87 123RF.com:** Alexutemov (tc). **Dreamstime.com:** Levente Gyori (bl). **88-89 Alamy Stock Photo:** Yolanda Oltra (t). **Dreamstime.com:** Jin Peng (Background). **88 Alamy Stock Photo:** Hilary Morgan (crb). **89 Alamy Stock Photo:** TCD / Prod.DB (cb). **90 Dreamstime.com:** Trekandshoot (cr). **Getty Images:** Jamie McDonald (r). **91 123RF.com:** lzflzf (ca). **Alamy Stock Photo:** Brian Lowe / ZUMA Wire (cb). **92-93 iStockphoto.com:** Lorado (t). **93 Alamy Stock Photo:** Dinodia Photos (ca); Janine Wiedel Photolibrary (cla). **94 123RF.com:** Allan Swart (cl, cr). **94-95 Dreamstime.com:** Adam88x (cb/Background); Albund (t/Background). **95 123RF.com:** Allan Swart (c). **Dreamstime.com:** Oocoskun (crb, bc). **96 Getty Images:** moodboard (cl). **97 Dreamstime.com:** Astrofireball (cra). **Getty Images:** Thomas Northcut / Photodisc (cla).

98 **Dreamstime.com:** Parkinsonsniper (br). **Getty Images:** The Asahi Shimbun (bc). 99 **Alamy Stock Photo:** Stephen Barnes (tl); Sueddeutsche Zeitung (cr); Barry Lewis (br). 102 **Dreamstime.com:** Beat Glauser / Hoschi (Background). 103 **Alamy Stock Photo:** Hiroyuki Sato / AFLO (cb). **Dreamstime.com:** Danyliuk (tr); Miramisska (tl). 104 **Dreamstime.com:** Gibsonff (cb); Miramisska (cb/Snowman). 104-105 **123RF.com:** Pakhnyushchyy (Background). 105 **Getty Images:** Kim Stallknecht (tr). 106 **Getty Images:** Alexander Hassenstein / Bongarts. 107 **Dreamstime.com:** Artisticco Llc (cl). **Getty Images:** Jonathan Nackstrand / AFP (br); Adam Pretty / Bongarts (tr). 108 **Getty Images:** Daniel Milchev (c). 108-109 **Getty Images:** Laurent Salino / Agence Zoom (cb). **iStockphoto.com:** Evilknevil. 109 **Dreamstime.com:** Andreykuzmin (tr). **Getty Images:** Tom Pennington (crb). 110 **Getty Images:** Dean Mouhtaropoulos - International Skating Union (ISU) / ISU (clb); Christof Koepsel - International Skating Union (ISU) / ISU (cb). 111 **Alamy Stock Photo:** Newscom (cra). **Dreamstime.com:** Vladimir Kulakov (c). **Getty Images:** Tim De Waele (clb). 112-113 **123RF.com:** Marina Scurupii (cb). 112 **123RF.com:** Dmitry Kalinovsky (cr). **Alamy Stock Photo:** Nordicphotos (cl). 113 **Alamy Stock Photo:** Everett Collection Inc (cra); Peter Horree (tl). **Getty Images:** Stanislav Krasilnikov\TASS (tc). 114-115 **123RF.com:** Jon Schulte (c/Background). **Alamy Stock Photo:** ITAR-TASS News Agency. **Dreamstime.com:** Martinmark (cb/Background). **Getty Images:** Gabriel Bouys / AFP (t/Background). 114 **Alamy Stock Photo:** Lorraine Swanson (clb). 115 **Alamy Stock Photo:** Michael Bush (cr). 116 **iStockphoto.com:** Dmytro Aksonov. 117 **Alamy Stock Photo:** imageBROKER (ca, cra); Alexander Piragis (br). 118-119 **Dreamstime.com:** Martinmark. **Getty Images:** Henning Bagger / AFP (c). 119 **Getty Images:** Gary M Prior / Allsport (tr). 122 **123RF.com:** Aleksey Satyrenko (cr). **Getty Images:** Alessandro Garofalo / Action Plus (c). 122-123 **Getty Images:** The Asahi Shimbun. 123 **123RF.com:** Benoit Daoust (tr); Aleksandr Markin (cr). **Alamy Stock Photo:** Westend61 GmbH (cl). **Getty Images:** Huw Fairclough (tc). 124-125 **Dreamstime.com:** Tanwalai Silp Aran (t); Issaranupong Chaimongkol / Imooba (b/Background). **Getty Images:** Ferenc Isza / AFP (ca); David Eulitt / Kansas City Star / Tribune News Service (cb). 126 **123RF.com:** Vladimir Ovchinnikov (l). **Dreamstime.com:** Tropicdreams (cr). 127 **Alamy Stock Photo:** Calamy Stock Images (cr). **Dreamstime.com:** Epicstock. 128 **Alamy Stock Photo:** Artokoloro Quint Lox Limited (cl). **Getty Images:** James Worsfold (clb). 128-129 **Getty Images:** James Worsfold. 129 **Alamy Stock Photo:** Cavan (crb). 130-131 **Getty Images:** Leo Mason - Split Second / Corbis. 131 **Getty Images:** Ullstein Bild (tr). 132-133 **Alamy Stock Photo:** Hero Images Inc.. 133 **Alamy Stock Photo:** Allstar Picture Library (cra). 134-135 **Depositphotos Inc:** geoffchilds. 135 **Alamy Stock Photo:** Tasfoto (tr). **Getty Images:** Jean-Michel Andre / AFP (cr). 136 **123RF.com:** Epicstockmedia (br). 137 **Dreamstime.com:** Mike K. / Mikekwok (br). 140 **Alamy Stock Photo:** Cavan Images (cr). **Bridgeman Images:** Egyptian / Fitzwilliam Museum, University of Cambridge, UK (bl). 141 **Alamy Stock Photo:** Age Fotostock (cb); Historic Collection / World History Archive (tr). **Bridgeman Images:** Aztec, (16th century) / Private Collection (cla). 142 **123RF.com:** smokhov (c/Background). **Dreamstime.com:** Sabelskaya (cb). 143 **123RF.com:** smokhov (bl). **Dreamstime.com:** Wavebreakmedia Ltd (bc). 144 **123RF.com:** PaylessImages (bc). 145 **Dorling Kindersley:** Natural History Museum, London (tr, cr); Stephen Oliver (crb, br). 146 **Alamy Stock Photo:** kpzfoto (clb). 146-147 **Alamy Stock Photo:** Findlay. 148-149 **Getty Images:** Matthias Hangst / Bongarts. 150 Dreamstime.com: Dodgeball (crb). 151 **Alamy Stock Photo:** MBI (l, cr). **Dreamstime.com:** Dodgeball (tr);

Monkey Business Images (c). 152 **Fotolia:** DenisNata (ca). 153 **Alamy Stock Photo:** Granger Historical Picture Archive (cra). 154 **123RF.com:** Rattasaritt phloysungwarn (cl, bc). 155 **Dreamstime.com:** Andersastphoto (br); Axel Bueckert (cra). 156 **Alamy Stock Photo:** Granger Historical Picture Archive (cla); KEYSTONE Pictures USA (c). **Getty Images:** Wally McNamee / Corbis (cra). 157 **Dreamstime.com:** Paul Topp / Nalukai (cra). 158 **Getty Images:** Popperfoto (bl). 159 **Dreamstime.com:** Sergey Rusakov / F4f (cra). **Getty Images:** Keystone-France / Gamma-Keystone (cla); Stephen Pond (crb); Simone Kuhlmey / Pacific Press / LightRocket (cb). 160 **Dreamstime.com:** Dmitry Pichugin / Dmitryp (clb). 161 **Alamy Stock Photo:** Granger Historical Picture Archive (t); Newscom (clb). 162-163 **iStockphoto.com:** Nosyrevy (b). 162 **Getty Images:** Wally McNamee / Corbis (bl). Rex by Shutterstock: Paul Vathis / AP (cr). 163 **PunchStock:** Westend61 / Rainer Dittrich (tr). 164 **Getty Images:** Norman Potter / Central Press (tr). 165 **Alamy Stock Photo:** KEYSTONE Pictures USA (l). 166-167 **Alamy Stock Photo:** Everett Collection Inc (c). 167 **Alamy Stock Photo:** INTERFOTO (crb); Pictorial Press Ltd (cl); United Archives GmbH (cr). **iStockphoto.com:** Nosyrevy (b). 168 **Getty Images:** DEA / Biblioteca Ambrosiana (crb). 169 **Alamy Stock Photo:** Keystone Press (t); Science History Images (tr). **Getty Images:** Scott Peterson / Liaison (crb); National Motor Museum / Heritage Images (clb). 170 **Dreamstime.com:** RightFramePhotoVideo (tl). 170-171 **Dreamstime.com:** Paul Topp / Nalukai. **iStockphoto.com:** Kerrick (t/Background). 171 **iStockphoto.com:** YinYang (cr). 172-173 **Dreamstime.com:** Reinhold Leitner / Leitnerr (Background). 172 **Alamy Stock Photo:** Science History Images (bc). 173 **Getty Images:** Hilaria McCarthy / Daily Express / Hulton Archive (br); Photo12 / Universal Images Group (c); General Photographic Agency (tr); Sandra Mu (b). 174 **Getty Images:** Ben Stansall / AFP (ca); Allsport Hulton / Archive (cla); Denis Doyle (cl); Stanley Weston (bc); TPN (br). 175 **123RF.com:** Olga Besnard (r). **Dreamstime.com:** Monner (ca); Sergeyoch (b). 176-177 **Getty Images:** TPN. 177 **123RF.com:** Oksana Desiatkina (crb). **Dreamstime.com:** Sergeyoch (cb). **Getty Images:** Adam Pretty (cl). 178 **Alamy Stock Photo:** AF archive (r). 179 **Dreamstime.com:** Alhovik (tr); Pincarel (tc); Julián Rovagnati / Erdosain (cra); Excentro (c). 180 **Getty Images:** Elsa (cl). 181 **Dreamstime.com:** Monner. 182 **Alamy Stock Photo:** Action Plus Sports (cl). 182-183 **Alamy Stock Photo:** Mauro Dalla Pozza (crb). 183 **Alamy Stock Photo:** Pacific Press Agency (crb). 184 **Dreamstime.com:** Olga Besnard. 185 **123RF.com:** Olga Besnard (c). **Dreamstime.com:** Igor Dolgov (clb). 186-187 **Getty Images:** Ben Stansall / AFP. 187 **123RF.com:** Adamgolabek (tl). **Getty Images:** Simon Maina / AFP (ca); Steve Turner (crb). 188 **Getty Images:** Al Bello (clb). 188-189 **Getty Images:** Tom Pennington. 189 **Getty Images:** Alex Menendez (bl). 190 **Getty Images:** Jerry Cooke / Sports Illustrated (cl); Chris Ratcliffe (crb). 191 **Getty Images:** Stanley Weston (cl). 192-193 **Alamy Stock Photo:** Xu Chang / Xinhua. 193 **Dreamstime.com:** Pariyawit Sukumpantanasarn (br). 194 **Getty Images:** Denis Doyle (r). 194-195 **Dreamstime.com:** Raja Rc / Rcmathiraj. 195 **Alamy Stock Photo:** Pau Barrena / Xinhua (cla). 196 **Getty Images:** Allsport Hulton / Archive (r). 196-197 **iStockphoto.com:** Kerrick (t/Background). 197 **Dreamstime.com:** Stephen Noakes (br). **Getty Images:** Paul Kane (clb). 198-199 **Getty Images:** Chris Elise / NBAE (b). 198 **Alamy Stock Photo:** Michael Mcelroy / ZUMA Wire (tl). 199 **Alamy Stock Photo:** Storms Media Group (tc). 200-201 **Getty Images:** Leontura (t). 200 **Alamy Stock Photo:** Everett Collection Inc (cra). Pedro Ugarte / AFP (bl). 201 **Getty Images:** Chris Graythen (cla); Vladimir Rys (ca). 202 **Alamy Stock Photo:** Archive Pics (crb); Jan Miks (tr). **Getty Images:** Shirley Kwok / Pacific Press / LightRocket

(cl). 203 **Dreamstime.com:** Lars Christensen / C-foto (cla); Idey (cla/Stadium). **Getty Images:** Streeter Lecka (bl). 204 **Getty Images:** Harry How (crb). 204-205 **Dreamstime.com:** Jin Peng (c/Background). 205 **Alamy Stock Photo:** Karl-Josef Hildenbrand / dpa (c). 206 **Alamy Stock Photo:** George S de Blonsky (bl). **Getty Images:** Peter Stone / Mirrorpix (cl). 206-207 **Alamy Stock Photo:** sportpoint (tl). 207 **Getty Images:** Scott Barbour / ALLSPORT (tr). 208 **Getty Images:** Vladimir Rys (l). 208-209 **123RF.com:** Kwanchai Chai-udom (t). **Alamy Stock Photo:** Santiago Vidal Vallejo (bc). **Dreamstime.com:** Raja Rc / Rcmathiraj (b/Background). 209 **Getty Images:** Reg Lancaster / Daily Express (tr); Vladimir Rys (cr); Wolfgang Kaehler / LightRocket (crb). 210 **Getty Images:** Pedro Ugarte / AFP (bl). 210-211 **Dreamstime.com:** Elena Chepik (Confetti). **Getty Images:** Gabriel Bouys / AFP (t/Background). 211 **Getty Images:** Christopher Morris / Corbis (b). 212 **123RF.com:** xsight (r). 213 **123RF.com:** Baiba Opule (cb). **Alamy Stock Photo:** Jason Pohuski / CSM (br); Dan Anderson / ZUMAPRESS.com (cra). **Dreamstime.com:** Jakub Gojda (cr); Guido Vrola (c). **Getty Images:** Christopher Evans / MediaNews Group / Boston Herald (cl); Burazin / Photographer's Choice RF (tl); Robin Alam / Icon Sportswire (bl). 214 **Getty Images:** Michael Allio (cl). 214-215 **Getty Images:** Michael Allio / Icon Sportswire (Background). 215 **Getty Images:** Bettmann (bc/Al Unser); Chris Graythen (ca); Michael Allio / Icon Sportswire (c); Bob D'Olivo / The Enthusiast Network (bc); Focus on Sport (br). 216 **Alamy Stock Photo:** Graham Morley Historic Photos (bc). 216-217 **Alamy Stock Photo:** Jon Sparks (cra). 217 **Alamy Stock Photo:** The Picture Art Collection (cra); Jan de Wild (br). 218 **123RF.com:** Leonard Zhukovsky (clb). **Alamy Stock Photo:** imageBROKER (crb). **Getty Images:** Jean-Loup Gautreau / AFP (bc). 219 **Alamy Stock Photo:** Everett Collection Inc (bc); PCN Photography (cr); Trinity Mirror / Mirrorpix (ftr); imageBROKER (clb). **Dreamstime.com:** Trentham (clb). 220 **123RF.com:** Alexutemov (tr). **Alamy Stock Photo:** Lucy Calder (br). **Getty Images:** Manuel Blondeau / Icon Sport (bc). 221 **Getty Images:** Nao Imai / Aflo (bc). 222 **Getty Images:** The Asahi Shimbun (bc). 223 **Getty Images:** Visual China Group (tl). 224 **123RF.com:** martinkay78 (br). **Alamy Stock Photo:** Action Plus Sports (bc). **Dreamstime.com:** Vladimir Galkin (bl)

Cover images: *Front:* **Alamy Stock Photo:** Action Plus Sports cra; **Dreamstime.com:** Skypixel cla; *Back:* **Alamy Stock Photo:** Cultura Creative (RF) cra; **Dreamstime.com:** Astrofireball cla, Idey cl, Stephen Noakes crb, Oocoskun tc

All other images © Dorling Kindersley
For further information see: www.dkimages.com

DK would like to thank:
Martin Copeland and Lynne Murray for picture library assistance, and Marie Lorimer for indexing.